# INTERMEDIATE 2

# English

## Jane Cooper

Close Reading Consultant: **Ann Bridges**

HODDER
GIBSON
AN HACHETTE UK COMPANY

The Publishers would like to thank the following for permission to reproduce copyright material:

**Photo credits** Page 49 (top left) © Popperfoto/Alamy, (top right) © Topham Picture Point/Topfoto; page 130 © Hodder Gibson; page 160 (left) © Northern Lights Cover Illustration: Dominic Harman/Arena; Reproduced with the permission of Scholastic Ltd All Rights Reserved, (right) © reprinted by permission of The Random House Group Ltd; page 161 (left) © Cover of "Different Seasons" by Stephen King with permission of Hodder Publishing, (right) © Cover of "Knots and Crosses" by Ian Rankin with permission of Orion Books, an imprint of The Orion Publishing Group; page 206 © Topham /Photri/Topfoto; page 212 © Anna Natalie Bennett.

**Acknowledgements** Extracts from exam papers and SQA letters of instruction reprinted by permission of the Scottish Qualifications Authority; In the Snack Bar from Collected Poems by Edwin Morgan (1996) reprinted by permission of Carcanet Press Ltd; 'Great Yarmouth Express' by Petra Regent reprinted by permission of Anvil New Poets (Anvil Press Poetry Ltd 1990); 'From the Motorway' © Anne Stevenson, Poems 1955-2005 (Bloodaxe Books, 2005); 'The Visitors' reprinted by permission of Sarah Reynolds. First published in 'Queen of the Sheep: New Writing Scotland 23', Thornton, Valerie and Whyte, Hamish (eds.), ASLS, Glasgow 2005.; 'Why Homework Isn't Working' by Anushka Ashtana Copyright Guardian News & Media Ltd 2007; 'The Great Horse Chestnut Mystery' (New Scientist), taken from Does Anything Eat Wasps? Reproduced by permission of Profile Books; 'Where have all the sparrows gone?' by Michael McCarthy from The Indypendium: A Celebration of 20 Years of Independent Journalism Part 2 1996-2006, published by The Independent (2006) and reprinted with permission.; Extract from AS I WALKED OUT ONE SUNDAY MORNING by Laurie Lee (Penguin Books, 1971) Copyright © Laurie Lee 1969; Slummy Mummy by Fiona Gibson, published in the Sunday Herald (21st January 2007) and reprinted by permission of the author; 'This Britain' by Brian Jackman taken from The Sunday Times Bedtime Book; 'We may yearn to be green, but we can't afford to be gullible' by Max Hastings Copyright Guardian News & Media Ltd 2007; The Test by Angelica Gibb Copyright © 1940 Condé Nast Publications. All rights reserved. Originally published in The New Yorker. Reprinted by permission.; 'Death of a Spinster' taken from Walking Wounded by William McIlvanney; If I Quench Thee reproduced by permission of William E Chambers; 'Local Colour' from Dreaming Frankenstein by Liz Lochhead is reproduced by permission of Polygon, an imprint of Birlinn Ltd (www.birlinn.co.uk); MY PARENTS KEPT ME FROM CHILDREN WHO WERE ROUGH, from NEW COLLECTED POEMS by Stephen Spender © 2004. Reprinted by kind permission of the Estate of Stephen Spender.; 'Telephone Conversation' Copyright © Wole Soyinka. Reproduced by permission of the author c/o Rogers, Coleridge & White Ltd., 20 Powis Mews, London W11 1JN.; from The Family Tree by Carole Cadwalladr, published by Black Swan. Reprinted by permission of The Random House Group Ltd.; Misadventures in a White Desert by Patrick Woodhead; extract from Toast reprinted by permission of HarperCollins Publishers Ltd © Nigel Slater 2003; extract from The Almond Blossom Appreciation Society by Chris Stewart reproduced by permission of Sort of Books; Extract from Heaven Knows I'm Miserable Now by Andrew Collins, published by Ebury. Reprinted by permission of The Random House Group Ltd.

Every effort has been made to trace all copyright holders, but if any have been inadvertently overlooked the Publishers will be pleased to make the necessary arrangements at the first opportunity.

Although every effort has been made to ensure that website addresses are correct at time of going to press, Hodder Gibson cannot be held responsible for the content of any website mentioned in this book. It is sometimes possible to find a relocated web page by typing in the address of the home page for a website in the URL window of your browser.

Hachette's policy is to use papers that are natural, renewable and recyclable products and made from wood grown in sustainable forests. The logging and manufacturing processes are expected to conform to the environmental regulations of the country of origin.

Orders: please contact Bookpoint Ltd, 130 Milton Park, Abingdon, Oxon OX14 4SB. Telephone: (44) 01235 827720. Fax: (44) 01235 400454. Lines are open 9.00–5.00, Monday to Saturday, with a 24-hour message answering service. Visit our website at www.hoddereducation.co.uk. Hodder Gibson can be contacted direct on: Tel: 0141 848 1609; Fax: 0141 889 6315; email: hoddergibson@hodder.co.uk

Cover photo © Nick Hanna/Alamy
Illustrations by Ian Heard/Redmoor Design
Typeset in 12 on 14pt Bembo by Phoenix Photosetting, Lordswood, Chatham, Kent
Printed in Italy

A catalogue record for this title is available from the British Library

ISBN-13: 978 0 340 94629 9

Impression number     5 4 3 2
Year                            2012  2011  2010  2009

# Contents

*The CD-ROM contains:*

Textual Analysis: Marking Guidelines

Close Reading: Marking Guidelines

The Intermediate 2 course gives you many opportunities to display your English skills. You will be assessed in class and also by an exam at the end of the course.

The four assessments you tackle in class are usually called **NABs** (National Assessment Banks). You can do these NABs in any order, and your teacher will decide when you are ready to each one. They are:

- **Textual Analysis**, in which you are given a short piece of literature text that you have never seen before and have to analyse the writer's skills and techniques

- **Close Reading**, in which you read a short passage of non-fiction and answer questions on it

- the **Personal Study**, in which you choose a book to study, and then plan and write an essay about it

- **Writing**, in which you plan and produce a story, a piece of personal writing, a discursive piece or some other piece of writing.

Once you have passed all the NABs you will be ready for the exam, which will take place in mid-May. There are two exam papers:

- **Close Reading**, in which, as with the NAB, you read a non-fiction passage and answer questions on it

- The **Critical Essay**, in which you write two essays about literature texts you have studied in class

This book contains everything you need for a complete Intermediate 2 English course, including three poems and three short stories you can study to prepare for the critical essay exam. (Your teacher may also use other literature texts, perhaps a play or a novel.)

Once you've finished this course you may want to go on to Higher. That course is harder, but it does follow the same structure as Intermediate 2 and assess the same skills, so what you're about to do now will be a good preparation for the future too.

# 1 Textual Analysis

The **Textual Analysis** NAB is based on an extract from a short story, novel or play, or perhaps on a whole short poem. You have to read the text carefully, and then answer questions on **how** it is written – the techniques the writer uses and the effects he or she creates.

Your Textual Analysis skills will also be useful in the Close Reading NAB and final Close Reading exam, where some questions will be marked with an **A** to show they are testing these skills. The Textual Analysis NAB also overlaps with your study of literature. When you study a literature text you are really analysing it, and whenever you use the ITQEE structure (which you can learn about later in this book) to write about a text, you are being analytical.

Writers choose every single word very carefully. They use a number of **language techniques**. These techniques are also sometimes called the **features** of the text, or **aspects** of the text.

In this chapter you will learn to look carefully at the writer's:

- **word choice**: the words the writer deliberately uses
- **structure**: the way the writer builds up sentences, or paragraphs, or the whole text
- **imagery**: for example **simile, metaphor** and **personification**, in which the writer describes something by **comparing** it to something else, giving you a vivid **image** or picture in your mind

and a number of other techniques.

Just to remind you what these mean, we'll examine them by using examples from the poem 'In the Snack Bar' by Edwin Morgan. This poem tells a story, and you should be able to understand it fairly easily at first reading.

 **WARNING**   We will just use this poem to illustrate some techniques. This is not the same thing as studying the poem, and it doesn't necessarily mean that you will end up knowing it well enough to be able to write about it in your exam.

## In the Snack Bar

A cup capsizes along the formica,
slithering with a dull clatter.
A few heads turn in the crowded evening snack-bar.
An old man is trying to get to his feet
5    from the low round stool fixed to the floor.
Slowly he levers himself up, his hands have no power.
He is up as far as he can get. The dismal hump
looming over him forces his head down.
He stands in his stained beltless gaberdine
10   Like a monstrous animal caught in a tent
in some story. He sways slightly,
the face not seen, bent down
in shadow under his cap.
Even on his feet he is staring at the floor
15   or would be, if he could see.
I notice now his stick, once painted white
but scuffed and muddy, hanging from his right arm.
Long blind, hunchback born, half paralysed
he stands
20   fumbling with the stick
and speaks:
'I want – to go to the – toilet'

It is down two flights of stairs, but we go.
I take his arm. 'Give me – your arm – it's better,' he says.
25   Inch by inch we drift towards the stairs.
A few yards of floor are like a landscape
to be negotiated, in the slow setting out
time has almost stopped. I concentrate
my life to his: crunch of spilt sugar,
30   slidy puddle from the night's umbrellas,
table edges, people's feet,
hiss of the coffee machine, voices and laughter,
smell of a cigar, hamburgers, wet coats steaming,
and the slow dangerous inches to the stairs.
35   I put his right hand on the rail
and take his stick. He clings to me. The stick
is in his left hand, probing the treads.
I guide his arm and tell him the steps.
And slowly we go down. And slowly we go down.
40   White tiles and mirrors at last. He shambles
uncouth into the clinical gleam.
I set him in position, stand behind him

And wait with his stick.
His brooding reflection darkens the mirror
45  but the trickle of his water is thin and slow,
an old man's apology for living.
Painful ages to close his trousers and coat –
I do up the last buttons for him.
He asks doubtfully, 'Can I – wash my hands?'
50  I fill the basin, clasp his soft fingers round the soap.
He washes, feebly, patiently. There is no towel.
I press the pedal of the drier, draw his hands
gently into the roar of the hot air.
But he cannot rub them together,
55  drags out a handkerchief to finish.
He is glad to leave the contraption, and face the stairs.
He climbs, and steadily enough.
He climbs, we climb. He climbs
with many pauses but with that one
60  persisting patience of the undefeated
which is the nature of man when all is said.
And slowly we go up. And slowly we go up.
The faltering, unfaltering steps
take him at last to the door
65  across that endless, yet not endless waste of floor.
I watch him helped on a bus. It shudders off in the rain.
The conductor bends to hear where he wants to go.

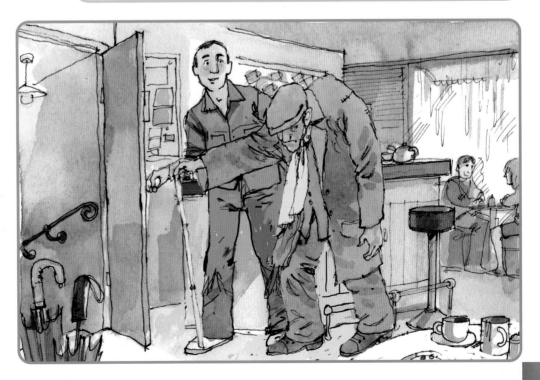

> Wherever he could go it would be dark
> and yet he must trust men.
> 70   Without embarrassment or shame
> he must announce his most pitiful needs
> in a public place. No one sees his face.
> Does he know how frightening he is in his strangeness
> under his mountainous coat, his hands like wet leaves
> 75   stuck to the half-white stick?
> His life depends on many who would evade him.
> But he cannot reckon up the chances,
> having one thing to do,
> to haul his blind hump through these rains of August.
> 80   Dear Christ, to be born for this!
>
> **Edwin Morgan**

# Imagery

Imagery is the term we use whenever a writer creates a picture in language. If the words a writer uses immediately create a picture in your mind, then you've just encountered an image. Some imagery techniques have particular names. Three of these are **simile**, **metaphor** and **personification**.

## Simile

A simile is a figure of speech in which one thing is compared to another using **like** or **as**. This gives a more vivid picture because of the similarity between the two things compared. For example:

> **Like a monstrous animal caught in a tent**
> **in some story.**

This suggests the size of the man, and shows how badly deformed he is as his disability has made him seem animal rather than human. Comparing his gaberdine coat to a tent shows that it seems ill-fitting and looks wrong on him.

Later in the poem, still describing the old man, Morgan notes his:

> **hands like wet leaves**

## Now try this

What image does this suggest in your mind about the man's hands? Write your own sentence(s) starting with these words:

*The simile 'hands like wet leaves' suggests . . .*

## Now try this

There's another simile near the start of the second verse. Find it, and write your own explanation of it as above.

## Metaphor

A metaphor is a comparison in which one thing is said to be another thing. Although this isn't true, it makes a strong comparison. For example:

> **That child is a pain.**

> **Her room is a rubbish dump.**

You won't find any metaphors in this poem, but you can find examples of metaphors elsewhere in this book in the chapter on 'Death of a Spinster'.

Similes are easy to spot but metaphors are much more difficult. They do not always use the word **is**. (The one in 'Death of a Spinster' doesn't.) Sometimes we have to ask ourselves if what the writer is saying can be literally true.

## Now try this

Pair up with someone you know quite well. Create five metaphors to describe your partner. Swap metaphors and see if you agree with each other's descriptions. **Then** choose one of the metaphors you created for your partner and try to explain the picture or image suggested by it. Write your own sentence(s) starting:

The metaphor (quote it) suggests . . .

## Personification

In this figure of speech, an inanimate, non-living, object is written about as if it was a **person** or a living creature. For example:

> **The dismal hump**
> **looming over him forces his head down.**

Can the hump on his back be pushing and forcing him? Of course not – it is not a living creature. Morgan is suggesting the hump **seems** alive because it looks as though it has deliberately pushed the man out of shape.

## Word choice

Of course all words that a writer uses are chosen in some way, but when we talk about **word choice** as a technique we mean that certain words are very carefully and deliberately chosen to obtain particular effects.

## Now try this

Answer the following questions about some of the word choice in the poem.

1 What can we tell about the snack bar from the fact that the old man's stool is 'fixed to the floor'? (Line 5)

2 What effect is created by the writer's use of 'dismal' in line 7?

3 What effect is created by the writer's description of the man's gaberdine coat as 'stained, beltless' in line 9?

4 What effect is created by the writer's use of the word 'fumbling' in line 20?

5 Why does the writer use the word 'contraption' to describe the hand drier in line 56?

# Figures of speech which involve sound

## Onomatopoeia

When a word **sounds like** what it is describing, we call this **onomatopoeia** Words like *thud, bang, splash, yawn* and *howl* are all examples of this technique. Most onomatopoeic words are to do with either sound or movement. An example in the poem is:

**slithering with a dull clatter**

Onomatopoeia is used to make the writing sound more vivid.

## Now try this

Look at the quotation above. Which is the onomatopoeic word? In what way does that word's sound suggest its meaning? Write your own sentence(s) starting:

The word (quote it) suggests . . .

## Alliteration

When letters or sounds are repeated at the beginnings of words we call this **alliteration** For example:

**A <u>c</u>up <u>c</u>apsizes along the formica**

Alliteration makes you notice the words more and draws your attention to what the writer is saying.

## Now try this

Look at the above line from the poem. What effect does the alliteration in this line have? Why do you think the writer began his poem this way? (This use of alliteration is very similar to the one that opens the poem 'Local Colour' later in this book.)

# Structural techniques

## Sentence structure

Often Textual Analysis or Close Reading questions ask you to examine **sentence structure**. You may be wondering where to start. First, you will only be asked about the structure of a sentence if the examiners think there is something noticeable or unusual about it, so you can start by asking yourself these questions:

**Length:**

- Is the sentence noticeably short or long?
- What effect does this length have?

**Sentence type:**

- Does the sentence make a statement?

  **She's a good girl.**

- Is the sentence in the form of a question?

  **Is she a good girl?**

- Is it an exclamation?

  **Good girl!**

- Does it give a command or instruction?

  **Be a good girl for your granny.**

- Is the sentence in the form of a list?
- What effect does the sentence type have?

**Word order:**

- Have the words been placed in an unusual order?
- What effect does this have?

**Grammar:**

- Would the sentence make sense on its own, out of context?

- Is it a minor sentence, one without a verb?

**She was a really good girl. Sometimes. Not always.**

(Minor sentences, while not grammatically perfect, can often make a big impact. Writers can use them to add drama or emphasis.)

- What effect does the grammar of the sentence have?

**Finally, ask yourself:**

- Is there anything else unusual about the way the sentence is written?

## Punctuation

Punctuation is part of sentence structure since it is used to shape sentences and to organise the words within them. To be able to answer punctuation questions, you need to know what common punctuation marks are used for:

**,**  **comma** separates short items in a list; or, if used in a pairs, can act the same way as dashes or brackets to mark off extra but non-vital parts of a sentence; or can indicate a pause or breathing place in the sentence

**:**  **colon** often used to introduce a list, a quotation, an idea, information, an explanation or a statement

**;**  **semi-colon** separates longer phrases within lists; or connects two different but linked ideas together to make one sentence

**—**  **dash** can be used in a pair like brackets to set aside information which isn't vital, or may be used singly to introduce a piece of information; can also indicate a pause

**' '**  **inverted commas** go round the exact words said when someone speaks **OR** go round the words quoted when a quotation is used **OR** can imply that something is only 'so called' and not genuine

**( )**  **brackets** used to separate off information which is interesting but not vital. The writing would still make sense if the bracketed part was missed out completely

**. . .**  **ellipsis** dots used to tail off a sentence or to show gaps in speech or writing

## Now try this

Look again at the poem and find:

A   At least three examples of dashes being used to create pauses. Quote each one, and explain why the writer wanted pauses there.

B   At least two examples of commas being used to create lists. Quote each one, and then explain why the writer used a list at that point.

### Repetition

Repetition is another structural technique: when a writer deliberately uses a word or phrase more often than you would normally expect. One example of repetition in this poem is:

> **'And slowly we go down. And slowly we go down.'**

This also slows down the reader, making us pay more attention to the repeated words. Here, the repetition suggests the difficulty of the journey down the stairs.

## Now try this

Read lines 57 to 65 of the snack bar poem. Find two more examples of repetition. In each case, quote them, and explain what effect Morgan gets by using that technique here.

## Contrast

A **contrast** is a form of opposite. Whenever you get a question about contrast, to get full marks you need to look at both sides. It's not a contrast to say

> **Jane is short and middle aged**

but it is a contrast if you say

> **While Jane is short and middle aged, Kenny is tall and young.**

## Now try this

Read lines 63 to 65 of the poem. The writer twice uses contrasting, opposite pairs of words.

■ How can the old man's steps be at once 'faltering' and 'unfaltering'?

■ How can their journey across the floor be at once 'endless' and 'not endless'?

■ What overall effect does Morgan create by using contrasts in this way?

## Attitude

Our **attitude** is how we feel about something, our opinion of it or reaction to it. A writer's attitude is often shown through other techniques, and you may need to read quite a large chunk of text before you can work out what the attitude is.

## Now try this

Re-read the poem. Then write a mini essay to explain the writer's attitude to the man he helps. Use the opening below to help you, and back up the attitude identified with quotations from the poem.

The writer's attitude towards the older man is that he feels sorry for him, yet in a way also admires him. . .

## Endings

You will often be asked why the ending of a text is suitable. This might involve looking at the last line(s) of a poem, or the last sentence or paragraph of a prose text. Endings can be suitable in a number of ways. For example:

■ the ending may sum up what the writer has been saying

■ the ending may emphasis a point made in the text

■ the ending may be humorous

■ the ending may give the reader something to think about

■ the ending may refer neatly back to something found earlier in the text

## Now try this

We are going to look at the ending of the poem in two ways.

1  Read the whole of the last verse. In what ways is this a suitable ending to the poem? You answer should be a paragraph and you should use some quotations from that verse to justify what you say.

2  Focus on the final line. In what way is this a suitable ending to the poem?

## Practising textual analysis

The rest of this chapter contains three Textual Analysis exercises for you to try. Each one is worth 30 marks, just like the NAB you will eventually sit. At the end of each question you will see the number of marks available. This will let you know how much to write in each answer. One exercise is on prose, and two get you to work with poems. The exercises get slightly harder as they go along.

In this poem the writer reflects on the effect of modern building developments on the countryside.

## The Great Yarmouth Express

Families already exhausted by the early hour,
Children sticky with too many bribes,
Slump in the heat of the fly-ridden train.
Strangers smile, finding
5    Their sufferings and expectation shared.

The train rumbles.
Sun lacquers the city we leave behind.
Fields lie, sculptured by the wind,
Burnished by the sun –
10    A still-life at sea, the green waves
Poised in defiance of natural law –
Until the harvest brings them down.

Beyond the window, the tide
Of new houses spreads –
15    Never recedes,
Like a fatal disease.
Preserving perhaps a few chosen things
Stranded on the future's shore:
A weed-choked stream, or straggling copse,
20    The church where mossed graves
Will soon be manicured and mown.

But at the seat of infection
In the city we've left behind,
An invading army silently
25    Stakes its claim.
The pioneers are already here –
Silken parachutes of willowherb descend
To colonize wasteland and crumbling stone.
Ragwort appears at bus-stops overnight.
30    Bindweed slips
Through cracks in paving stones,
And covers them in blooms of white.
Graffiti of anarchist and tyrant alike
Are replaced by the hieroglyphics
35    Of the vegetable world.
The tide of builder's rubble and earth
Spills like a dark wave upon a field
Lost to tomorrow's child.
But in the city's decaying heart,
40    An emerald forest grows.

**Petra Regent**

## Textual Analysis questions for 'The Great Yarmouth Express'

1  How does the word choice in verse 1 (lines 1–5) suggest that the train journey was going to be unpleasant? You should consider at least **two** examples.  **4**

2  Show how imagery connected with art is used in lines 6–10 to give a positive impression of the scenery. You should consider **two** examples. **4**

3  Choose one image from lines 13–16 and show how it creates a negative view of new housing developments.  **2**

4  Lines 17–21 suggest that the planners will try to 'preserve' some aspects of the countryside scene. Show how word choice **and** sentence structure suggest that these attempts will be not be very successful.  **4**

5  Show how the imagery in lines 22–23 helps to lay the blame for the new housing on the city.  **2**

6  The image of an army is developed in lines 24–28. Show how this extended image is effective in showing what weeds are doing to cities.  **4**

7  Read lines 29–35. Do you feel that the picture created of cities in these lines is attractive or unattractive? Referring closely to these lines give evidence for your answer.  **4**

8  (a) Look at the last verse (lines 36–40). How does the writer make you see a contrast between what is happening in the countryside and what is happening in the city?

You should consider **two** of the following techniques: word choice, sentence structure, imagery.  **4**

(b) What do these lines reveal about the writer's attitude to the developments in the countryside?

Quote the line which, in your opinion, first signals this attitude earlier in the poem.  **2**

**Total 30 marks**

In the next poem the writer is reflecting, sometimes in a light-hearted way, about the tyranny of the motorway system.

## From the Motorway

Everywhere up and down the island
Britain is mending her desert;
marvellous we exclaim as we fly on it,
tying the country in a parcel,
5    London to Edinburgh, Birmingham to Cardiff,
no time to examine the contents,

thank you, but consider the bliss of
sitting absolutely numbed to your
nulled mind, music when you want it,
10   while identical miles thunder under you,
the same spot coming and going
seventy, eighty times a minute,

till you're there, wherever there
is, ready to be someone in
15   Liverpool, Leeds, Manchester,
they're all the same to the road,
which loves itself, which nonetheless
here and there hands you trailing

necklaces of fumes in which to be
20   one squeezed breather among
rich and ragged, sprinter and staggerer,
a status parade for Major Roadworks
toiling in his red-trimmed triangle,
then a regiment of wounded orange witches

25   defending a shamelessly naked
(rarely a stitch of work on her)
captive free lane,
while the inchlings inch on
without bite or sup, at most
30   a hard shoulder to creep on,

while there, on all sides,
lie your unwrapped destinations,
lanes trickling off into childhood
or anonymity, apple-scented villages
35   asleep in their promise of being
nowhere anyone would like to get to.

Anne Stevenson

## Textual Analysis questions for 'From the Motorway'

1 Quote the words which show that the image of the motorways as 'tying' is extended in lines 4–6. What picture of the motorways is the writer trying to give you by the use of this imagery? **4**

2 Show how word choice in lines 7–12 helps to convey the monotony of motorway driving. You should consider **two** examples in your answer. **4**

3 How does the writer, in lines 13–16, use structure to emphasise what seems to her to be the sameness of places reached by the motorway? **2**

4 Show how the imagery in lines 18–20 is effective in suggesting the conditions of a traffic jam. **2**

5 What does line 21 tell you about the kinds of people or vehicles stuck in the traffic jam and how does the writer emphasise this? **2**

6 Explain why the phrase 'Major Roadworks' in line 22 creates a humorous effect. **2**

7 In lines 22–27 the description of the roadworks plays with or extends the 'Major Roadworks' image. Identify **two** words or phrases where this happens and show how they are effective in portraying the nuisance of the roadworks in a humorous or ironic way. **4**

8 Show how word choice in lines 28–30 highlights the slowness of progress through the roadworks. You should consider **two** examples in your answer. **4**

9 How does the writer's word choice in lines 31–36 suggest that 'off motorway' places are more pleasant? **2**

10 (a) What do you feel the writer's attitude is to motorways? Give evidence from the poem to back up your answer. **2**

(b) What is odd about the punctuation of the poem? What effect do you think the poet is trying to achieve by this use of punctuation? **2**

**Total 30 marks**

In the following short story an old man, who is now living in a residential home, has a visit from two of his adult grandchildren.

## The Visitors

He sits in the garden, waiting. Waiting and waiting for time to roll over him, for ninety-one summers to become ninety-two, ninety-three, ninety-four.

He says, 'I know your face lassie . . . and yours,' and, 'is that a wee bird or a leaf?'

He says, 'They're nice enough to you here. It's a lovely day.'

5 We watch together, the three of us. We watch the sky move and the trees sway and the boy in the mower hum in and out of the beds and shrubs leaving billiard green grass behind him.

We say, 'Are you comfortable here? Is the food good?'

10  He says, 'They're nice enough to you,' then hesitates, kneading at the knitted tammy in his lap with one hand, soothing the curved neck of his cane with the other. His fingers become slower and

15  slower on the marled wool. He is reading it. 'I don't know where she went. All dressed in frills and that, I don't know why she was all dressed up like that. I kissed her . . . and, I cuddled her. She

20  went down like a bag of potatoes. I wish it was me.'

No-one has any words. There are Livingston daisies laughing in the borders. Redwood trees like rocket ships keeling further towards you the longer and harder you look up. Clamouring birdsong, a Red Admiral flirting in and out of the roses.

25  'I don't know what she had to go and do that for.'

His shirt is all faded to winter, over a clean vest. Once it was vivid – royal blue with crimson tramlines. His belt is hauled tight, holding him up.

'I know your face.'

'We brought you a wee half-bottle, Papa. And some biscuits.'

30  'Oh aye. You needn't have bothered with me. I like a wee snifter though. There's a bottle in my room, it's still got that much in it.' He gestures two inches. 'I know your . . .'

'I'm your granddaughter!' I repeat, too quickly, too loudly, too much angst in my voice. I gush on, talking desperate rubbish, and at the mention of a dog he lights up. The dog leads him to everything – names, faces, cars, places; those who visit, those who don't; the

35  people he never talks to and the woman who sings all the time.

'She's a bloody nuisance, her.' He grins. The grin is meddling, young.

Bloody nuisances, me and my brother in a lost world of grand-childhood, combing beaches and his patience. Salt wind in our faces and a dizzy sky, we slip and slither on the rocks in stout Clark's sandals and his hands keep us from falling off the edge of the world. Gran on

40  a striped fold-down chair with her knitting needles clicking, keeping watch over the shell-studded castles and moats. I can't be in this place any more.

When we make moves to go, he lifts his face for a kiss. And this man who used to lift me up to the clouds cannot lift himself from the chair. He shrugs our help away and we follow him under low ceilings and dull lights through a maze of empty armchairs. He stops to

45  consider every turn, looking for clues to room 5. There's a reproduction case clock standing against the modern wall like a reluctant sentry. The pendulum swings without disturbing

the peace. In the bedroom he points to a framed picture on his otherwise barren dressing table. He puts his tammy down next to it.

50 'Aw Mamie. Seventy years. Seventy years together and she goes down just like that. I've a house just down the road. I've a mind to go there . . . I think it's empty. I've a mind to go there but on your own it's not the same. It's nice enough here.'

Our feet scrunch on the gravel on the way to the car. 'He's looking well,' we say, and leave the air heavy with other thoughts.

55 On the road back to the motorway we pass the graveyard. I can't look round. I hold onto myself and say hello to her away in the back of my mind. I look down and my knuckles are white. I wonder where the clock from that house along the road went, I used to listen to its heartbeat in my tightly tucked bed.

I look up and the sky is blue on blue. Cloudless. I don't know why she had to go and do that either.

**Sarah Reynolds**

## Textual Analysis questions for 'The Visitors'

1 Explain **one** way in which the writer in lines 1–2 makes you feel that the old man has an emptiness in his life.　2 A

2 Read lines 10–21.

(a) How does the language of lines 11–16 ('kneading at . . . reading it.') demonstrate in his actions the idea of 'then hesitates,'?

You should consider word choice **and** imagery in your answer.　4 A

(b) Why is the hesitation effective in giving impact to the important memory in the paragraph?　1

3 Show how the word choice **or** imagery of lines 22–24 ('There are Livingston daisies . . . in and out of the roses') creates a lively atmosphere in contrast with the sadness of what goes before and after it.　2

4 Read lines 26 and 27.

Show how **one** item in the physical description of the old man gives an impression of his mental outlook.　2

5 Read lines 32–39.

(a) Show how the sentence structure in lines 32–36 reflects the emotional state of the granddaughter.　2

(b) How does the sentence structure **or** word choice of lines 33–35 give a more positive impression of the grandfather?　2

(c) Show how the phrase 'bloody nuisances' in line 37 acts as a link in the granddaughter's line of thought.　2

6 Read lines 37–41.

(a) Quote a word or a phrase which shows the protectiveness of the grandfather **or** the grandmother in the past when the narrator and her brother were children. **1**

(b) Explain why the last sentence in this paragraph (line 41) is an effective ending to the paragraph. **2**

7 Show how word choice in lines 42–48 gives a disturbing impression of

(a) the home **2**

and

(b) the grandfather's state of mind. **2**

8 Explain the importance of **two** of the following in the story as a whole:

■ the use of the phrase '. . . nice enough here' (lines 4, 10, 51)

■ the 'tammy' in lines 12 and 48

■ the mention of clocks in lines 45–46 and in lines 56–57

■ the state of the weather in lines 5–7 and in line 58. **4**

9 How effective is the last sentence as a conclusion to the story? **2**

**Total 30 marks**

⚠ Your teacher will decide when you are ready for the NAB. Until then, get all the practice you can. Textual Analysis is a wide-ranging skill. This one chapter can't ever let you practise for all the questions you might meet. Your teacher may use other textbooks with you too, and may get you to practise with other tasks before you attempt the final NAB.

# 2 Close Reading

You have to pass a NAB in Close Reading and it will also be one of your two exam papers. This makes up 50% of your final grade. Close Reading passages are always about 1,000 words long, non-fiction and in prose. In recent years, these have been extracts from good newspaper articles, travel books and autobiographies. You get an hour for this task. Close Reading exercises are worth 30 marks and use three types of question:

- **Understanding** questions test your grasp of **what** the writer has written

- **Analysis** questions make you identify **how** the writer has written it

- **Evaluation** questions test you on **how well** you think the writer has written.

There will be a code letter (**U**, **A** or **E**) alongside each question to let you know what type of answer is required.

If you are really serious about passing, one of the best things you can do is *start reading more NOW!*

- Try to regularly read a good newspaper like the *Scotsman, Herald, Guardian* or *The Times*. Don't just read the news stories near the front, but also the feature articles and opinion pieces in the later pages.

- Read a biography or autobiography of a famous person.

- Read travel books in which writers describe interesting experiences in unusual places.

Read so that you can follow the argument in a piece of writing – that is, the writer's main line of thought. Try summarising this with bullet points.

Read so that you understand what the writer is saying – sometimes you can work out unfamiliar words from the context; at other times you may need to use a dictionary. You will not be able to take one into the exam, so it's important to work on building up your vocabulary.

# Understanding

## Explain in your own words

**Understanding** questions often ask you to **use your own words**. You may have to:

- explain what a word or expression in the passage means

- explain the main point the writer is making

- give the reason for something that happens in the passage

- show that you understand a piece of information the passage gives.

Read the following article about the value of homework which appeared in the *Observer* newspaper.

# WHY HOMEWORK ISN'T WORKING

## Leading academic says too much study after school turns children off education and sparks family rows

Amelia Warren, a nine-year-old from Maidstone, Kent, knows about homework. It is 6.20pm by the time she gets home from her after-school club, but she still has to sit down to worksheets covering numeracy, literacy and spelling. <u>At the weekend she fits projects for her teacher in between dance lessons and football games.</u>

'It would really surprise you,' said her mother, Laura. 'Some nights she has sheets with 100 times tables. I don't want it to become a chore because it will put her off. I work full-time; I do not want the time we spend together to be me and her battling about homework.'

<u>*FAMILY TENSION* is just one of a string of negative effects of homework for young children,</u> according to an explosive new book which says much of it is pointless. The book, *The Homework Myth*, to be published in Britain in the spring, also says too much of it turns chil-

dren off education and does not make them do any better in tests.

The study, by American academic Alfie Kohn, has sparked a huge debate on TV and radio and in hundreds of newspapers. Last week it reached the Wall Street Journal, where <u>it was reported that some of America's most competitive schools were cutting or eliminating work beyond their gates.</u>

'What surprised me is not the downside of homework, but the fact there appears to be no *UPSIDE*,' said Kohn. <u>'No study has ever shown an academic benefit to homework before high school.'</u>

<u>In the UK, it has emerged that a handful of</u>

primary school headteachers have started to drop traditional styles of homework in favour of 'fun' activities and outings that parents and children can do together. One London school has swapped sums and endless spelling for museum trips and cookery tasks.

Even that is too much for Kohn, who will spend his year giving dozens of lectures calling for parents to 'organise' into groups and go into schools to demand changes. 'Kids should have the chance to relax after a full day at school,' he said. In Kohn's eyes, primary schoolchildren should do no more than read for pleasure when they get home.

Soon his message will reach the UK, where the government made homework compulsory nine years ago, starting at one hour a week for five-year-olds. It is likely to reject his arguments.

'Homework is an essential part of education,' said a Department for Education and Skills official. 'A good, well-organised homework programme helps children and young people to develop the skills and attitudes they will need for successful, independent life-long learning.'

It is a view shared by many parents. Andy Hibberd, co-founder of the support group the Parent Organisation, says his sons aged seven and nine benefit greatly from the work they bring home. 'When they go to secondary school, then further and higher education, they will have to do homework,' said Hibberd, from Wingworth, near Chesterfield, Derbyshire. 'I think for primary school children to start bringing home a little bit of homework so they are prepared is a good thing. It does not hurt younger children to do 10 minutes a day.'

However, a recent review by Susan Hallam, a professor at the Institute for Education in London, showed that setting the wrong type of work can be DETRIMENTAL to pupils. 'It needs to be meaningful,' said Hallam. 'If it is just being set as something schools feel they have to do with no real thought to its purpose, then it is a waste of time. Homework, if taken to the extreme, can completely disrupt family life.'

Some headteachers are SCEPTICAL too. 'Many teachers have long suspected homework wasn't beneficial for the children,' said John Peck, head of Peafield Lane Primary School in Mansfield, Nottinghamshire. 'Sometimes it is done more for the parents who demand it. It would be a brave school that decided to eliminate homework.'

At Coleridge primary school in north London, the head, Shirley Boffey, has replaced many aspects of traditional homework with 'home learning'. Sums, grammar and spelling have been reduced. Instead worksheets filled with ideas about making models, trips to museums, cookery and art are sent home.

One sheet suggests that parents take their children to nearby Alexandra Palace to look through the telescope; another asks them to make bread together; while one focuses on learning about the local area. 'We did it for all the reasons that they are arguing in the US,' said Boffey. 'We didn't feel homework was working, we wanted children to enjoy learning and not see it as a chore.'

Some parents love the new system; others are yet to be convinced. Vikki Poole, from Muswell Hill, has two daughters at the school, aged seven and 10, and loves the new system. Her girls took home 'very formulaic' work from their last school. Now the family gets together once a week to do the tasks and Poole loves the new system.

But for others, such as Ilana Wegrzyn, the new regime means extra stress. 'I have two boys, eight and 10. One may have to cook a curry and the other one bake bread. Each topic can take an afternoon. I work part-time, but with their music and sport it is a real pressure.'

Wegrzyn prefers more traditional homework, but she could not deny that her boys love the new work.

Anushka Asthana

This sentence from the first paragraph of the article:

**At the weekend she fits projects for her teacher in between dance lessons and football games.**

could also be expressed as:

**On Saturdays and Sundays she has to make time for homework between enjoying sports and other hobbies.**

## Now try this

Several other sentences in the article have also been underlined. Re-write each one in your own words. You don't have to change every single word, and you may find that some long sentences can be reworded better as two or even three shorter ones.

## Context questions

Sometimes a question asks you to work out from the **context** what a word or expression means. The examiners think that you probably will not know the given word, but that you can work it out from what surrounds it in the passage.

Here are some ways the examiners might ask context questions:

- Explain in your own words what is meant by _____ in this context.

- How does the context of lines _____ help you to work out what is meant by _____?

- Work out from the context what is meant by _____ in line _____.

You can learn a **formula** to help you answer these questions. Look at this extract from the news article:

**Amelia Warren, a nine-year-old from Maidstone, Kent, knows about homework. It is 6.20pm by the time she gets home from her after-school club, but she still has to sit down to worksheets covering numeracy, literacy and spelling. At the weekend she fits projects for her teacher in between dance lessons and football games.**

Now here's a possible question:

**How does the context of this paragraph help you to work out what is meant by 'homework'?**

As you can see, the word 'homework' in the passage is followed by a mention of Amelia doing 'worksheets' after she returns home. It also refers to her working on projects 'at the weekend'. This suggests the writer is using 'homework' to mean schoolwork done outside school hours. Here is a possible answer to the question:

*The expression 'homework' as used here means schoolwork that pupils do outside school hours. I can work this out from the context because the expression is followed with a mention of 'worksheets' done at home in the evening and projects done 'at the weekend'.*

Of course you already knew what the word 'homework' means. The example above is just to show you the method.

Context questions are usually worth two marks. You earn one mark for showing what the word means, and the second for showing how you could work this out from the context. Your answer should therefore be in two sentences, with the second including some short quotations from the context.

Use this pattern to structure your answers.

**The word/expression '_____' as used here means _____. I can work this from the context because ...**

## Now try this

Look back at the news article again. You will see some words printed in BOLD CAPITALS. Using the method and structure shown above, explain what each word means, and how that meaning can be worked out from the context. Remember the context clues may come before or after the word, and may not all be in the same paragraph as the word itself.

## Following the argument/line of thought

One of the most important things you need to be able to do in the Close Reading NAB and final exam is **follow the argument** This just means that you **understand the line of thought** in the writing. Following the argument involves more than just understanding the words. You need to be able to think about the words and understand the thoughts and ideas behind them. Some passages may contain just one argument, usually that of the writer, while others may present two or more opposing points of view.

### Now try this

Take a piece of paper, or a page of your notebook, and divide it in two from top to bottom. Label the left hand column 'Arguments against homework' and the right hand column 'Arguments in favour of homework'. Now read the news article again and, as you do so, note down the arguments for and against giving school children homework. Put each one in your own words as far as possible, and use bullet points to organise your lists.

### Now try this

The following short Close Reading task will allow you particularly to focus on **U** questions. The article relates the story of how children collected horse chestnuts, conkers, during the First World War.

### The Great Horse Chestnut Mystery

An entry in the local school logbook from the village of Nash in North Buckinghamshire, dated 9 November 1917 states 'Letter of thanks received from the Director of Propellant Supplies for chestnuts gathered for the making of munitions.'

5 Speculation led to thoughts of chestnut shrapnel, but this was obviously far-fetched. A more sensible answer focused on the use of chestnuts in the making of acetone which, in turn, was needed for the production of cordite, the smokeless powder used as the explosive propellant in small arms ammunition and artillery.

Smokeless powders such as cordite had changed the face of battle. They offered longer range than 'black powder' better known as gunpowder. Producing only a faint blue-grey
10 haze, they permitted machine guns to fire without obscuring the gunner's view and they permitted snipers to operate without revealing their position. Cordite is a mixture of the

explosives guncotton (65%), nitro-glycerine (30%) and petroleum jelly (5%), gelatinised with the aid of acetone.

15 Before the war acetone was produced almost entirely by the heating of wood in the absence of oxygen to distill the acetone vapour released. The world market for acetone was dominated by the great timber-growing countries like Russia and America, Britain's
20 acetone being mainly imported from the USA. At the outbreak of the First World War in August 1914, however, the stocks of acetone for military use stood at only 3,200 tons. It was soon apparent that production would not meet the rapidly growing
25 demand.

Pre-war techniques were inadequate to meet the needs of the wartime army. As minister of munitions, David Lloyd George appointed Chaim Weizmann, a chemist who had emigrated from mainland Europe in 1904, to increase acetone production using a process of his own invention involving the bacterial fermentation of maize starch. Factories at Poole in Dorset
30 and King's Lynn in Norfolk produced up to 90,000 gallons of acetone a year.

By 1917, however, the German submarine offensive in the Atlantic had caused a shortage of freight which threatened to cut off supplies of North American maize. With the consequent possibility of a serious maize shortage, experiments began to find a substitute. When it was discovered that the horse chestnut could be used as an alternative in acetone production,
35 schoolchildren were recruited to collect horse chestnuts and vast quantities were gathered. But only 3,000 tons reached the Kings Lynn plant. Collection was restricted by transport difficulties – letters to *The Times* tell of piles of rotting horse chestnuts at railway stations.

After initial engineering difficulties with the plant, the Kings Lynn factory began production of acetone from horse chestnuts in April 1918. Further difficulties to hamper manufacture
40 arose from the fact that the horse chestnut was a low-yield material from which to produce acetone. The plant was eventually closed in July 1918.

This explanation accounts for the 'chestnut' reference in Nash's school logbook.

A more lasting footnote to this episode in history – in Lloyd George's own words 'a permanent mark on the map of the world' – arose from Lloyd George's gratitude to Chaim
45 Weizmann. He was so grateful that, on becoming Prime Minister, he gave Weizmann direct access to the foreign secretary to lobby for an independent homeland for the Jewish people. The result was the famous *Balfour Declaration* of 2nd November 1917, stating that the British Government viewed with qualified favour 'the establishment in Palestine of a national home for the Jewish people'. When, much later, the state of Israel came into existence,
50 Weizmann was elected as its first president in 1948 and held that position until his death in 1952.

*Does Anything Eat Wasps?*

# Close Reading questions for 'The Great Horse Chestnut Mystery'

1 Read lines 1–7.

(a) From your reading of these two paragraphs give the meaning of 'propellant' **and** 'munitions'. **2**

(b) How does the context of **each** of these words help you to work out its meaning? **2**

(c) What was the first guess the writer had about the purpose of the chestnuts? Why did he discard this answer? **2**

2 Give **two** advantages that cordite has over gunpowder. (lines 8–14) **2**

3 Read lines 15–25.

Briefly state the **three** main points made about Britain's acetone in this paragraph. **3**

4 In your own words give the meaning of the sentence in line 26. **2**

5 How did the intervention of Chaim Weitzmann help the situation? **1**

6 Read lines 31–37.

(a) Briefly give **two** reasons for the campaign to collect chestnuts. **2**

(b) What reason is given for only 3,000 tons of chestnuts reaching King's Lynn? **1**

(c) What evidence is given to back up this reason? **1**

7 Read lines 38–41.

What **two** difficulties were faced in the King's Lynn factory in 1918? **2**

8 What does 'This explanation' (line 42) refer back to? **1**

9 Read lines 43–51.

(a) Why was Lloyd George grateful to Weitzmann, and what did he do to show his gratitude? **2**

(b) Why is this 'footnote' to the chestnut story a more important one than the entry in the Nash school logbook? **2**

**Total 25 marks**

## Analysis

Only about half of the questions you have to answer in Close Reading are marked with **U** to indicate an Understanding question. The others are marked with **A for Analysis** or **E for Evaluation**. In this book the chapter on Textual Analysis will give you lots of help in answering Analysis questions. For now, we will just focus on one particular **A** question type.

## Link questions

**Link questions** often ask you to say how a sentence **creates an effective link** between one paragraph and another. These questions are usually worth two marks and you usually need to answer them in two parts:

■ show how one part **links back** to the previous paragraph

■ show how the other part **refers forward** to the new paragraph.

For example, a **link question** based on the homework news article might be worded like this:

How does the sentence 'Family tension is just one of a string of negative effects of homework for young children, according to an explosive new book which says much of it is pointless.' form a link between paragraphs 2 and 3 of the article?

A good answer to this would be:

*The expression 'family tension' links back to the battles over homework mentioned in the previous paragraph.*

*The expression 'an explosive new book' introduces the book mentioned in paragraph three, ideas from which will be discussed in the rest of the article.*

This answer would get two marks because it has two parts to it, one linking back, the other referring forward. We can put this into a **formula for link questions** which, with occasional slight adaptation, should ensure you always get two marks for this question.

**The word/expression '_____' links back to _____ which was discussed in the previous paragraph.**

**The word/expression '_____' introduces the idea of _____ which is going to be discussed in the new paragraph.**

## Now try this

Answer the following link questions about the homework news article you read near the start of this chapter.

1   How does the first sentence of paragraph 7 'Even that . . . demand changes.' form a link between paragraphs 6 and 7?

2   How does the first sentence of paragraph 10 'It is a view shared by many parents.' form a link between paragraphs 9 and 10?

3   How does the first sentence of paragraph 11, 'However . . . detrimental to pupils.' form a link between paragraphs 10 and 11?

## Now try this

The following short Close Reading task will let you practise your skills in analysing **structure**. This will include both **sentence structure** and the **structure of the whole passage**.

Before you attempt it, it may help if you go back to Chapter 1, Textual Analysis, and revise the section on structure from there.

In the passage you are about to read, Michael McCarthy identifies a disturbing ecological mystery.

## Where Have all the Sparrows Gone?

The game of spot-the-difference begins almost
as soon as you get off the Eurostar at Gare du
Nord. It's irresistible: London and Paris are now
so close to each other on the surface; but in
5   subtle ways still so far apart. Walk along a
boulevard and pick out the things you just don't
see in London. Look at the number of women
wearing fur. Look at the number of women
walking small, chic dogs wearing fur . . . Look
10  how well the Metro runs. Look how clean the
streets are. Look at the sparrows.

Yes indeed, look! Sparrows! Here we are with the children on a half-term break last month,
buying an ice-cream at the Palais de Chaillot as we take in the stupendous view across the
river to the Eiffel Tower, and what's this around our feet? Half a dozen of them, cheeky,
15  chancing their luck, darting in for the dropped crumb, the piece of cornet. Here they are
scuffling crossly over the children's playground in the Tuilleries, here they are hopping with
intent along the formal walks of the Luxembourg Gardens, here they are hanging around
the little flower market on the Left Bank in a chattering flock.

Paris is full of sparrows. It always has been (the city's most memorable singer, small but
20  irrepressible, called herself after the French slang word for a sparrow, *Piaf*). But London isn't.
Not any more. In one of the most remarkable events in the natural world of the past few
decades, only now being properly perceived, the capital's sparrows have disappeared. Once
more cockney than the Cockneys, they are now a rarity in London.

At the Tower of London, in Trafalgar Square, at Piccadilly Circus, around Big Ben, outside
25  Buckingham Palace, in St James's Park, at any of the sites where tourists gather and where
twenty years ago hungry and hopeful sparrows would pursue them, just like their plentiful
Parisian cousins were doing last month, they have vanished.

Across central London, in the streets, under the eaves, in the hedges, along the railway lines,
in the great railway stations, in the parks and the gardens and the trees, they have melted
30  away.

They have. They've gone. No one understands why. All that can be said with certainty is that
within the London sparrow eco-system something mysterious, something catastrophic, has
taken place.

Michael McCarthy

# Close Reading questions for 'Where Have all the Sparrows Gone?'

1 Show how the sentence structure of 'It's irresistible . . . apart' (lines 2–4) helps to highlight the idea contained in 'the game of spot-the-difference'. **2**

2 Read lines 6–9.

Explain fully the effect of the writer's use of the phrase 'Look at . . .' in these lines. **4**

3 Why are the first two sentences (line 10) an effective opening to the second paragraph? **2**

4 Look again at lines 14–17.

What structural technique does the writer use to give you an impression that sparrows in Paris are plentiful? How does it do so? **2**

5 Show how the writer uses sentence structure in lines 18–21 (Paris is...any more) to create an effective contrast. **2**

6 Look at the structure of the sentence in lines 23–26. Explain **two** ways by which the writer makes it dramatic. **4**

7 Show how the same **two** techniques are used in the next paragraph (lines 27–29). **2**

8 Name **one** of the structural techniques used in the last paragraph and show how it adds to the effectiveness of the end of the article. **2**

**Total 20 marks**

## Now try this

The following short Close Reading task will let you practise your skills in analysing **imagery** and **word choice**.

Before you attempt it, it may help if you go back to Chapter 1, Textual Analysis, and revise the sections on imagery and word choice there.

In the passage you are about to read, Laurie Lee describes his journey over the Pyrenees to Spain where he hoped to join the International Brigade, fighting in the Spanish Civil War during the 1930s.

## Almost the Last Lap

Throughout the long clear morning I struggled up the mountain path, buffeted by icy winds from the north. The great peak of Canigou stood away to my right, floating in the brilliant sky like an iceberg, and, for much of the time, not having a compass, I was able to use it as a sighting post. By noon I had climbed to about 3,000 feet, but the goat track grew more

5  and more tortuous, so I decided to abandon it altogether and go straight up the mountain, still keeping Canigou on my right.

The way was tricky and hard, and I found myself stumbling on my knees and clawing at rocks and tufts of frozen grass. By the middle of the afternoon I was sweating in the cold, slipping and scrambling over the frozen slopes. But I was high up now, with a prickling

10  across the back of my neck as I felt the whole of France plunging away behind me. Having been born and brought up at two hundred and fifty feet above sea level, I was not used to such dizzying elevations.

Suddenly there was an ominous change in the atmosphere, an extra keenness of cold and a curious glare and whitening of the sunlight. Looking down, I saw that the foothills had

15  disappeared and had been replaced by a blanket of swirling vapour. The shining peak of Canigou began to switch on and off like a lighthouse, intermittently shuttered by the racing clouds. Then the wind rose abruptly to a thin-edged wail, and I felt the first stinging bite of snow.

One moment I'd been climbing a mountain in a sparkle of sunshine; the next, the whole

20  visible world had gone, and I was slapped to my knees and pinioned to a shelf of rock, head down in a driving gale. Gusts of snow swept round me, needling my eyelids and piercing my clothes like powdered glass. The storm closed in and began scouring the mountain with an insane and relentless frenzy.

For a while I curled myself up and became just a ball of survival, mindlessly hugging the

25  shelter of a rock. I lay knee to chin, letting the storm ride over me; then I began to wonder what I was doing here. After all the boasting I'd done in the summer fields back home, what was I doing in France stuck to the face of a mountain alone in a winter blizzard? To lie freezing to death on the wrong side of the frontier was no way to go to war. There was no point in staying where I was, so I started

30  to move forward, crawling slowly on hands and knees. Distance, direction, movement and balance were all fused together in my senses by the driving snow. All I remember is the brightness of the ground and being swept by waves of

35  almost infantile pleasure, the delirious warmth of impending frostbite.

Then, by one of those long-shot chances, taken for granted at the time, I came

40  upon a rough little stone-built shelter. It

was half in ruins, and there was nothing inside it but straw, but I suppose it may have saved my life. Once I had bedded myself down, I heard the blizzard change gear, rising to an almost supersonic shriek, and for a couple of hours I lay motionless, curled deep in the straw, slowly and painfully, thawing out.

45 Later it grew dark, and the anguish gradually eased as I built up a drowsy fug for myself. The sound of the wind settled down to a steady whine, sleepy, like an electric motor. A pleasant comfort crept over me; I seemed to sense the feather-soft snow gathering in deep drifts outside; a bosomy presence, invisible and reassuring, cushioning the naked rocks of the mountain. By now I was exhausted anyway, too drugged by the cold to move, even to
50 attempt to build a fire; so I just lay, sniffing the damp warm smell of the straw, and presently I fell asleep.

Next morning the storm was over and the sun shone brilliantly again. I came out of the dark little hut to find the mountain transformed – trees, rocks and bushes thickly bolstered with snow and giving off a clean, crispy smell, like starch. The French village below me was out of
55 sight, but the slope above curved gradually away, smooth and bright, rising a few hundred yards then ending in a sharp blue line of sky.

Abandoning the cosy gully where I'd spent the night, I climbed unsteadily for an hour or so until suddenly there was no more climbing; the slope levelled and stopped, the sky plunged, and I was on top of the ridge.

60 The icy crests of the Pyrenees stretched east and west, flashing in the sun like broken glass on a wall, while before me, to the south, was what I had come to see – range after range of little step-like hills falling away to the immensities of Spain…

Laurie Lee

# Close Reading questions for 'Almost the Last Lap'

1 What impression does the simile in line 3 give you of the appearance of Canigou? **2**

2 Choose **one** word or phrase from paragraph 2 (lines 7–12) which you feel to be particularly effective in emphasising the discomfort of his climb. Quote the word or phrase and then justify your choice. **2**

3 Show how the imagery in paragraph 3 (lines 13–18) emphasises the idea of 'an ominous change'.

You should refer to **two** examples in your answer. **4**

4 Show how word choice **and** imagery in lines 19–23 show the hostility of the storm. **4**

5 Why is 'fused' an appropriate word to use in line 32 to represent his feelings at that moment? **2**

6 Look at lines 38–44.

Show how imagery makes a contribution to the description of the sounds surrounding the hut. **2**

7 Show how the use of metaphor **and** simile in lines 45–51 leads up to the last statement in the paragraph 'presently I fell asleep'. **4**

8 Read lines 57–59.

Show how word choice **or** imagery in these lines gives an impression of what it felt like to reach the top of the ridge.

You should refer to **one** example. **2**

9 Read the last paragraph (lines 60–62).

(a) Show how 'The icy crests of the Pyrenees . . . broken glass on a wall' is effective in showing what the writer has achieved. **2**

(b) How effective do you feel the last lines of the passage ('range after . . . Spain . . .') are in providing an appropriate ending to this section of Lee's journey? Refer to particular words or phrases in your answer. **1**

**Total 25 marks**

## Evaluation

In Evaluation answers, you have to say how **good** or **effective** or **successful** or **appropriate** a particular piece of writing is. You may be asked for instance:

- to comment on the **effectiveness** of a technique the writer uses

- to explain how **effective** you consider the ending of a passage to be

- to show how well the writer **achieves his or her purpose**

- to explain how **convincing** the writer's arguments are

- to explain why you find the writer's style **enjoyable**

- to comment on how **effective** or **appropriate** the title of the passage is.

Evaluation questions tend to come towards the end of the task. The exam setters always think the passages they choose are well-written, so you can begin your answers with something like:

- This is effective because . . .

- This is a good technique here because . . .

You also have to **justify your answer**. In other words you have to give reasons for your answer. This should be based mostly on the text, and will involve quotation.

Read the following passage in which Fiona Gibson looks at the advantages and disadvantages of being 'really organised'.

## Slummy Mummy

1   I used to aspire to being extremely sorted. As sorted, in fact, as the Really Organised Women featured in the February issue of Easy Living magazine. One such woman, owner of a tote bag company, has the forethought to attach a strip of reflective tape – 'bought in a cycle shop' – to illuminate the inside of her handbag 'so I never struggle to find things'. Why stop at that? Why not have a little light installed, like you'd find in a fridge?

2   The trouble with such tips is that they invariably involve extra toil (in ten years of parenting, I have yet to get it together to stitch a name tape on to a child's garment, hence numerous lost coats). For instance, the same tote bag lady also sets time aside on a Sunday evening to plan what to wear for the entire week ahead, and makes notes.

3   The annoying thing is, I know she has a better time of it in the mornings than I do. She isn't raking through chaotic underwear drawers, and never discovers an escaped sock in the washing machine. She does indeed look highly efficient, perched in front of her shoes all stored in transparent boxes. But how realistic is this approach? Does such a highly efficient being ever have to sully her immaculateness by tackling really filthy jobs, like shoveling out a crust of bunny pellets from a hutch?

4   Surely such a level of organisation – deciding on Sunday that on Thursday you'll be wearing black trousers and a blue polka-dot shirt – does scary things to a person, such as sapping your spirit and propelling you to the conclusion that your existence, at least the fun part of it, is over.

5   I once worked with a woman who planned her family's menus a full month in advance. I'm sure it made sense, and created less waste – after all, the average family slings away around a quarter of the food that they buy – but who can predict that they'll fancy a prawn curry in 27 days' time?

6   One friend of mine runs a highly organised home – but then she also starts madly washing up while you're still eating your meal, and I have caught her polishing a light flex. Another High Priestess of Tidy Pants Drawers admits: 'I am organised in the extreme. I've been known to put post-it notes on dishes before a dinner party to remind me what food should go in it.'

7   If I am ever tempted to resort to such measures, please slap a Post-It on to my forehead on which you have written: KILL ME'.

Fiona Gibson

## Now try this

The first few questions on this passage allow you to work again on some **Understanding** questions. **Answer in your own words**.

1 Look at paragraph 2. What is the main 'trouble with such tips'?

2 Look at paragraph 3. What is an advantage of being organised?

 What doubt does the writer raise about being so organised?

3 Look at paragraph 4. What does the writer see as the disadvantage of 'such a level of organisation'?

4 Look at paragraph 5. What is the advantage of planning menus? What is the disadvantage of planning menus?

5 Look at paragraph 6. What two examples does the writer give of what she sees as over-organisation?

## Now try this

Now that you understand the passage well, answer these final questions to **evaluate** the writer's attitude and style.

6 Look at the first and the last paragraphs. What do you think the writer's real attitude to being 'really organised' is? Justify your answer by referring to word choice, sentence structure and tone in these paragraphs.

7 One of the purposes of this article is to entertain and amuse the reader. By referring to specific language features show how the writer has tried to be humorous.

## Now try this

To finish this chapter, you will now have two opportunities to work on full-scale, 30-mark, Close Reading tasks which cover all three question types. In the first passage Brian Jackman looks at the British countryside, its origins and its decline, and considers how this decline can be halted.

# This Britain

Homeward bound on Friday nights, I drive from Dorchester along the Roman road. The road strikes westward across high chalk downs, past mediaeval dew-ponds, stone- age burial mounds and twentieth century pylons. At one point it runs along the outer ramparts of an Iron Age hillfort. Then, abruptly, it drops over the chalk cliff, skirts a Saxon deer forest and

5    plunges through the hollow lanes of sandstone country to my home, a Domesday village with a Norman church.

There is nothing remarkable about this journey. It takes no more than twenty minutes. But that shortcut through this part of Dorset demonstrates everything that is best about the British landscape. For in the space of less than fifteen miles you cross the great divide

10    between two geological periods and span 3000 years of history.

In no other country has the face of the land been so deeply etched by centuries of continuous habitation. Nowhere else can you find such an extraordinary patchwork of different habitats in what is, after all, a fairly small island.

Britain doesn't go in for brash extremes. There are no deserts, no glaciers, no Niagaras or

15    Matterhorns. But that is not to say the British landscape lacks drama. For a demonstration of home-grown elemental savagery, walk out along any Cornish headland when a heavy sea is running. When heavy rollers charge the bays head on, and the shock of their fall, the suck and grind of pebbles swept up in their terrible undertow booms in the fissures and chasms of the shaken cliffs, then that coastline becomes the wildest place on earth.

20    And there are other places, as in the Black Cuillins of Skye, where even on a calm day, the silence of those implacable summits, the feeling of being watched by unseen eyes, is overpoweringly eerie.

Often it is a manmade feature which dominates the view: Bamburgh's hoary sea castle crouched on its rock above Northumbrian dunes; or the Uffington White Horse, that free-

25    flowing piece of pagan graffiti carved in the turf of the Berkshire Downs. It could hardly be otherwise in an island where man has been tilling, building, scratching and burrowing since the last Ice Age.

After the Norman Conquest in 1066, the pace of change quickened: the Mediaeval peasant beat back the forest with his bill-hook and ox-plough; the Norman Kings set aside vast

30    expanses of wilderness for hunting; the monasteries were responsible for draining tracts of fertile land. In Elizabethan times sheep took over the landscape changing the ancient design of fields. The next two centuries saw the effect of the Enclosure Acts which has given Britain its most characteristic texture: the orderly patchwork of chequered fields cross-hatched by hedgerows or, in the uplands, dry stone walls.

35    But change came at a price. Timber, the energy source of Elizabethan England, became scarce. The once inexhaustible woods were finally all but consumed, the native oaks devoured by iron-founders, ship-builders and expanding industry. Timber was replaced by seemingly unlimited supplies of coal in thick seams from Cardiff to the Clyde.

In the mid-eighteenth century, coal, water-power and the harnessing of steam came

40 together in the middle of Britain and the Industrial revolution was born. The Age of Steam brought hideous changes to the countryside. The green skin was ripped away to get at the coal beneath. The mines spewed out ghastly slag heaps. Towns and factories spread out into the fields, polluting the streams and poisoning the air. Canals were dug, farms were mechanised, the railways opened, and man's progress, until now geared to the pace of the
45 horse, spurted forward. The destruction of the countryside had begun.

The process has been accelerating ever since. Every advance of technology has required some sacrifice of precious land. Airports, oil refineries, overspill. Giant pylons shackle the supple symmetry of the landscape. Hedgerows are grubbed out to create monoculture prairies for the barons of agri-business. And so to our own motorway age, with the sinister
50 silhouettes of nuclear power stations beckoning us to who knows what kind of Britain.

Meanwhile, in spite of change, much of Britain remains untouched. Out there beyond the six-lane highways and sprawling cities you can still catch the pulse of an older, elemental Britain of badgers and hawks' nests, sphagnum bogs and salmon pools.

Today wild life and wild places are cherished as never before. A new spirit of environmental
55 awareness is in the air. Foul rivers are running clean again. Pioneers of conservation, among them the National Trust and Nature Conservancy Council are fighting to safeguard our finest landscapes and wildlife habitats.

The sum total is a rich and heady mixture: Scottish osprey lochs and wild Welsh uplands; moorland and mountain; Norfolk flint and Lakeland slate; potholes and precipices; national
60 park, heritage coast… The ancient fabric of Britain's countryside may lie in tatters but it still glitters with an irresistible magic

Brian Jackman

## Close Reading questions for 'This Britain'

1 Read lines 1–10.

   (a) What does the writer think are the **two** best aspects of the British landscape? **2 U**

   (b) Quote **one** detail from lines 1–6 which exemplifies **each** of these aspects. **2U**

2 Show how sentence structure **or** imagery in lines 11–13 emphasises his view that the British isles are uniquely marked as a result of human habitation. **2 A**

3 By referring to the imagery **or** word choice the writer uses in lines 15–19 show how the 'drama' of the Cornish coast is emphasised. **2 A**

4 Read lines 23–27.

   (a) 'Often it is a manmade feature which dominates the view'

   What reason does the writer give for this being the case? **1 U**

   (b) How does the sentence structure in these lines help to clarify the thought of the paragraph? **2 A**

5 Briefly state in your own words **four** of the changes which happened to the landscape after the Norman Conquest. **4 U**

6 Read lines 35–38.

'But change came at a price.'

What was the price? **1 U**

7 Read lines 39–45.

How do the imagery **and** word choice lead up to the conclusion that 'The destruction of the countryside had begun.' **4 A**

8 Show how the sentence 'Meanwhile, in spite of...remains untouched.' (line 51) acts as a turning point in the passage. **2 A**

9 Read lines 54–57.

By referring to particular words or phrases, show how these lines create a more hopeful view of the fate of the countryside. **2 A**

10 Read lines 58–61.

(a) Show how in lines 58–60, sentence structure illustrates the idea of a 'rich and heady mixture'. **2 A**

(b) What is the meaning of the last sentence 'The ancient . . . irresistible magic.' **2 U**

(c) How effective is this sentence in summing up the ideas of the passage? **2 E**

**Total 30 marks**

## Now try this

In this second task Max Hastings asks for more research into green remedies, such as wind-farms, instead of just assuming that any scheme the environmentalists put forward must be on the right track. This is a good example of a passage where the writer is putting forward an argument.

## We May Yearn to be Green, but We Can't Afford to be too Trusting

An independent study by the Renewable Energy Foundation declared at the weekend that most wind-farms in England are a waste of space. Government targets for wind-turbines assume that they will operate at 30% of capacity. Most work well below that, because their sites are insufficiently windy.

5 Businesses which put up wind-turbines beside their offices (not to mention politicians who put them on their houses) are erecting a garden ornament, not a power station. These wind-turbines are merely statements of good intentions; they are certainly not contributions to efficient generating capacity. They are also, of course, damnably ugly.

The study is not surprising to those of us who have believed all along that wind-turbine mania reflects an unholy alliance between ambitious manufacturers, greedy landowners and easily fooled politicians who are happy to lavish extravagant subsidies on doubtful technology because it polishes up their green credentials without costing anybody except the taxpayer, who, naturally, exists to be stuffed.

'Buying British' may be patriotic, but makes limited ecological sense. Lamb can be raised in New Zealand and sold in England for less energy-cost than producing it here. Winter tomatoes can be grown in Spain and trucked to British shops more energy-economically than by growing them under glass here.

These facts raise questions about the entire local organic-growing concept: ploughing land to destroy weeds may do more environmental damage through fuel use than spraying weedkiller. Some experts argue that a growing system based on sowing crops on the surface of the ground and using weedkiller is more sustainable than so-called 'organic' farming which is a doubtful and uncertainly-defined concept even on a good day.

Now, my purpose here is not to claim to be an expert on any of these issues. It is merely to suggest that we, as citizens, should be much more sceptical about quack remedies peddled in the sacred name of environmentalism.

Thoughtful people have reached a condition in which most of us want to behave better towards the environment than we have done in the past. We yearn to make our tiny contributions towards stemming the flood of global warming, and towards pursuing sustainable policies.

Unfortunately, however, it is much harder to do so than we want to think. There are sharks out there, dressed in shiny green camouflage suits, who want to persuade us that by buying this, not buying that, despoiling the landscape with turbines each bearing the Green seal of approval, we can 'do our bit' for the environment.

The truth, of course, is that, as with every divorce, there is no painless means of parting from our old life and embracing a new. Almost every significant improvement in the global environment will require international agreements made by governments, and savage taxes imposed on individuals to make them change their behaviour, above all in the use of fossil fuels. Only a tiny minority of people are willing – for instance – to drive less, unless obliged by cost to do so.

It does not seem fanciful to me, a military historian, to compare the current passion for erecting wind turbines with the building of RAF Blenheim bombers in 1939. You may not know that the Blenheim was a disastrous military aircraft, recognised to be so at the time.

50 Yet it was built in its hundreds, and rushed into service sending the planes and their hapless pilots almost seamlessly to extinction at the hands of the German Luftwaffe.

The thinking behind this folly was simple: it was 'better to build something than nothing'. In truth, of course, it was pointless to put into the air planes incapable of doing the business, as the pilots' widows agreed. The erection of wind farms in England costs no lives, but
55 represents the same thinking.

Sustainable energy we must have. Some of us pray nightly for the swift evolution of wave-power technology, offshore wind-farms, electric cars, improved water harvesting, and home insulation. But it represents expensive, landscape-wrecking madness to plant wind-turbines where there is not enough wind to make them economic – which means almost everywhere
60 in England.

Less damaging gestures such as organic food purchases, or biomass fuelled cars, at least enable consumers to signal to the world that they care. Climate change frightens many of us, including me.

It is because so many people are now waving green flags that some politicians are jumping
65 on the bandwagon. However cynical their motives, if more of them start thinking green, there is some small hope for us all. But please: unless, or until, the numbers add up, let's have no more subsidised, futile wind-turbines which look satanic beside the M4 and silly on top of houses in the suburbs.

**Max Hastings**

# Closed Reading questions for 'We May Yearn to be Green'

1 Read lines 1–4.

What reason does the writer give for calling wind-farms 'a waste of space'? **1 U**

2 Read lines 5–8.

Show how the structure of the sentence beginning 'These wind-turbines . . . generating capacity' helps you to understand the first sentence 'Businesses . . . power station'. **2 A**

3 Read lines 9–19.

(a) Which **three** groups of people does the writer suspect of acting together to promote wind-turbines at the expense of the taxpayer? Answer in your own words as far as possible. **3 U**

(b) Show how word choice **or** imagery in these lines conveys his disapproval of these groups and their activities. **2 A**

4 (a) Show how 'These facts raise questions about the entire local organic-growing concept:' (line 25) acts as a link in the passage. **2 A**

(b) Identify **two** ways in which the writer creates a tone of doubt about the benefits of organic farming in lines 27–29. **2 A**

5 Read lines 30–36.

(a) Look at the introduction to the passage on page 67 and then, in your own words give the meaning of the sentence 'It is merely . . . name of environmentalism' (lines 30–32).  **2 U**

(b) Show how word choice in the last sentence of the paragraph 'We yearn to . . . sustainable policies' emphasises how much 'we want to behave better towards the environment . . .'  **2 A**

6 Identify **one** example of imagery from lines 37–40 and show how it emphasises how difficult it is to avoid being misled about environmental issues.  **2 A**

7 Read lines 41–46.

What **two** things are necessary to make the world change to follow a more sustainable path?  **2 U**

8 Read lines 46–51.

Show how the anecdote about the Blenheim bombers is relevant to the writer's main concern in the passage.  **2 A**

9 Show how the sentence structure in lines 56–60 helps to promote the writer's strong views.  **2 A**

10 Read lines 64–68.

(a) What hope **and** what warning are included in this paragraph? Use your own words in your answer.  **2 U**

(b) Show how imagery **or** word choice is used to highlight **either** the hope **or** the warning.  **2 A**

(c) From your reading of the whole passage, do you feel that the writer has used language effectively to promote his dislike of wind-turbines in England? You should refer to specific words, phrases or sentences in your answer.  **2 E**

**Total 30 marks**

You've now practised most of the language techniques and types of questions needed to pass the Close Reading NAB and Close Reading paper in the SQA exam. Your teacher will decide when you are ready to attempt this NAB. Until then get as much practice as you can. You may get the chance to do similar tasks from other textbooks, and to use past exam papers too.

# 3 Prose: The Test

The three genres of literature you can write about in the exam are **drama**, **poetry** and **prose**. Writing about **drama** involves showing your knowledge and understanding of the script of a play. We can't cover that in this book, as there isn't space to include and study an entire drama text. You will find three pieces of **poetry**, and work to go with them, later in this book. First, though, we are going to study some **prose**.

**Prose** just describes any piece of writing that is written in sentences and paragraphs. In the Intermediate 2 course the two sorts of **fictional prose** that you might study are **novels** and **short stories**.

 ## Getting in

You're about to read a short story. It follows a woman taking her driving test. Before you read the story, think about the following questions. You should share your answers with a partner, a small group or your class.

- Would you describe yourself as good or bad at passing tests and exams?

- How do you feel when you know you have some sort of test coming up?

- Have you ever been given a test that you felt was unfair?

 ## Meeting the text

As you read through the story for the first time, make two lists:

1. List all the times the driving inspector calls Marian by the wrong name. Each time, take a note of the paragraph number and of the name he calls her.

2 List all the times the driving inspector uses what he thinks is a southern accent, or a southern dialect or expression. Each time note the paragraph number and then quote what he says.

## The Test

1 On the afternoon Marian took her second driver's test, Mrs Ericson went with her. 'It's probably better to have someone a little older with you,' Mrs Ericson said as Marian slipped into the driver's seat beside her. 'Perhaps the last time your cousin Bill made you nervous, talking too much on the way.'

2 'Yes, Ma'am,' Marian said in her soft unaccented voice. 'They probably do like it better if a white person shows up with you.'

3 'Oh, I don't think it's *that*,' Mrs Ericson began, and subsided after a glance at the girl's set profile. Marian drove the car slowly through the shady suburban streets. It was one of the first hot days in June, and when they reached the boulevard they found it crowded with cars headed for the beaches.

4 'Do you want me to drive?' Mrs Ericson asked. 'I'll be glad to if you're feeling jumpy.' Marian shook her head. Mrs Ericson watched her dark, competent hands and wondered for the thousandth time how the house had ever managed to get along without her, or how she had lived through those earlier years when her household had been presided over by a series of slatternly white girls who considered housework demeaning and the care of children an added insult. 'You drive beautifully, Marian' she said. 'Now, don't think of the last time. Anybody would slide on a steep hill on a wet day like that.'

5 'It takes four mistakes to flunk you,' Marian said. 'I don't remember doing all the things the inspector marked down on my blank.'

6 'People say they only want you to slip them a little something,' Mrs Ericson said doubtfully.

7 'No,' Marian said. 'That would only make it worse, Mrs Ericson, I know.'

8 The car turned right at a traffic signal into a side road and slid to the curb at the rear of a short line of parked cars. The inspectors had not arrived yet.

9 'You have the papers?' Mrs Ericson asked. Marian took them out of her bag: her learner's permit, the car registration, and her birth certificate. They settled down to the dreary business of waiting.

10 'It will be marvellous to have someone dependable to drive the children to school every day,' Mrs Ericson said.

11 Marian looked up from the list of driving requirements she had been studying. 'It'll make things simpler at the house, won't it?' she said.

12 'Oh Marian,' Mrs Ericson exclaimed, 'If only I could pay you half of what you're worth!'

13 'Now, Mrs Ericson,' Marian said firmly. They looked at each other and smiled with affection.

14  Two cars with official insignia on their doors stopped across the street. The inspectors leaped out, very brisk and military in their neat uniforms. Marian's hand tightened on the wheel. 'There's the one who flunked me last time,' she whispered, pointing to a stocky, self-important man who had begun to shout directions at the driver at the head of the line. 'Oh Mrs Ericson.'

15  'Now Marian,' Mrs Ericson said. They smiled at each other again, rather weakly.

16  The inspector who finally reached their car was not the stocky one, but a genial, middle-aged man who grunted broadly as he thumbed over their papers. Mrs Ericson started to get out of the car. 'Don't you want to come along?' the inspector asked. 'Mandy and I don't mind company.'

17  Mrs Ericson was bewildered for a moment. 'No,' she said, and stepped to the curb. 'I might make Marian self-conscious. She's a fine driver, Inspector.'

18  'Sure thing,' the inspector said, winking at Mrs Ericson. He slid into the seat beside Marian. 'Turn right at the corner, Mandy-Lou.'

19  From the curb, Mrs Ericson watched the car move smoothly up the street.

20  The inspector made notations in a small black book. 'Age?' he inquired presently, as they drove along.

21  'Twenty-seven.'

22  He looked at Marian out of the corner of his eye. 'Old enough to have quite a flock of pickaninnies, eh?'

23  Marian did not answer.

24  'Left at this corner,' the inspector said, 'and park between the truck and the green Buick.'

25  The two cars were very close together, but Marian squeezed in between them without too much manoeuvering. 'Driven before, Mandy-Lou?' the inspector asked.

26  'Yes, sir, I had a license for three years in Pennsylvania.'

27  'Why do you want to drive a car?'

28  'My employer needs me to take her children to and from school.'

29  'Sure you don't really want to sneak out nights to meet some young blood?' the inspector asked. He laughed as Marian shook her head.

30  'Let's see you take a left at the corner and then turn around in the middle of the next block,' the inspector said. He began to whistle 'Swanee River.' 'Make you homesick?' he asked.

31  Marian put out her hand, swung around neatly in the street and headed back in the direction from which they had come. 'No,' she said, 'I was born in Scranton, Pennsylvania.'

32 The inspector feigned astonishment. 'You-all ain't Southern!' he said. 'Well dog my cats if I didn't think you-all came from down yondah.'

33 'No, sir,' Marian said.

34 'Turn onto Main Street and let's see how you-all does in heavier traffic.'

35 They followed a line of cars along Main Street for several blocks until they came in sight of a concrete bridge which arched high over the railroad tracks.

36 'Read that sign at the end of the bridge,' the inspector said.

37 '"Proceed with caution. Dangerous in slippery weather."'

38 'You-all sho can read fine,' the inspector exclaimed. 'Where d'you-all learn to do that, Mandy?'

39 'I got my college degree last year,' Marian said. Her voice was not quite steady.

40 As the car crept up the slope of the bridge the inspector burst out laughing. He laughed so hard he could scarcely give his direction. 'Stop here,' he said, wiping his eyes, 'then start 'er up again. Mandy got her degree did she? Dog my cats.'

41 Marian pulled up beside the curb. She put the car in neutral, pulled on the emergency brake, waited a moment and then put the car into gear again. Her face was set. As she released the brake her foot slipped off the clutch pedal and the engine stalled.

42 'Now, Mistress Mandy,' the inspector said, 'remember your degree.'

43 '*Damn* you!' Marian cried. She started the car with a jerk.

44 The inspector lost his joviality in an instant. 'Return to the starting place, please,' he said, and made four very black crosses at random on the squares on Marian's application blank.

45 Mrs Ericson was waiting at the curb where they had left her. As Marian stopped the car, the inspector jumped out and brushed past her, his face purple. 'What happened?' Mrs Ericson asked, looking after him with alarm.

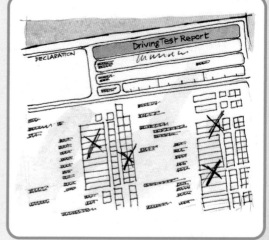

46 Marian stared down at the wheel and her lip trembled.

47 'Oh Marian, *again*?' Mrs Ericson said.

48 Marian nodded. 'In a sort of different way,' she said, and slid over to the other side of the car.

Angelica Gibb

## Thinking through

First, share your answers to the 'Meeting the Text' questions you were given at the start of the story. Then work out the answers to the following three questions:

1   When is the first point in the story where we realise that Marian is black and the other characters are white? How do we know this?

2   Why does Marian keep failing her driving test?

3   In your opinion, would she have passed if Mrs Ericson had gone along in the car with them?

 ## Let's get to work

This story is obviously about injustice, prejudice and racism. The author, Angelica Gibb, doesn't tell us what to think about these serious issues. She doesn't tell us what she thinks either. Instead she puts her message across by showing how the issues affect one person on one day. As we study this story we are going to look especially at how the author creates the main character, Marian, and at the ways in which Marian relates to and is contrasted with the other characters. Remember that, while Marian is black, everyone else in the story is white.

## Setting

Before we go on to look at Marian and the other characters, it will help you to understand the story if you have a clear idea of the time and place in your mind.

### Now try this

First of all, answer this question:

1   Which country do you think the story is set in?

You should have found that question easy to answer, but do you know how you worked it out? It's because certain words and phrases scattered throughout the story gave you clues.

Some of these clues were **dialect** words, words that belong to the kind of English spoken in a certain place.

2  Which word used in paragraph 5 tells you the story is set in that country?

3  Which word used in paragraph 35 tells you the story is set in that country?

Some of the words were factual.

4  Which word used in paragraph 24 tells you the story is set in that country?

5  Which word used in paragraphs 26 and 31 tells you the story is set in that country?

You should even be able to work out if the story is set in the north or the south of this country.

6  Look at paragraphs 30 and 32. Which area of the country is this story set in?

Now that we've dealt with the **place setting** of the story, we also need to work out **the time setting**. This is harder to do, and the story only gives us one clue for this.

7  Look at paragraph 31. What does Marian do which drivers do not need to do nowadays?

One more question:

8  Did you spot anything else in the story that helped you work out the place or time setting?

All these answers help us to put the story in a historical context. Marian is a young black woman living in one of the northern states of the USA. The fact that she has to put out her hand to signal when she turns in the road shows that she is driving a car made before indicator lights became standard. (It can't be that she owns an old car. The car is not hers. It belongs to her employer who is rich enough to employ staff and not to need to have a job of her own. Mrs Ericson would own a fairly new car.) This puts the story in perhaps the mid to late 1950s.

America was a much more racially divided country in those days. The situation was much worse in the southern states but even in the north, where the story is set, few good jobs were open to black people. Not many black people had any education beyond school. The big civil rights movements of the 1960s, and black leaders like Martin Luther King and Malcolm X, were not yet active. Although black people in America were strongly aware of the injustice around them, there was very little they felt they could do about it.

Martin Luther King

Malcolm X

# Marian

All of this makes Marian a very striking character. Nowadays if you met a 27-year-old with a degree who was working as a housekeeper you might think they should be making more of themselves, or following a more challenging career. But Marian has managed to get a degree at a time when it would have been very hard for any black person to do so. University education in America has never been free, so she must have had to work before she was at college, and probably also while she was there, to pay for her studies. Also, in the time the story is set, even white women often did not go on to study after leaving school. Marian must have had to challenge many people's prejudices and assumptions to get

as far as she has already. Angelica Gibb wants us to admire Marian, and to dislike the driving inspector. It's part of how she puts across her message about racism in the story.

That's one explanation of why Marian deserves our respect. Gibb also presents her as someone who is skilled, and aware. There is lots of evidence throughout the story that Marian is actually a very good driver. Once we know all of this evidence, it becomes even clearer to us that the Inspector is a racist who treats Marian unfairly. He fails her because she is black, and because he is not going to let a black woman get away with snapping at him.

49

## Now try this

Read through the story. Every time you find a piece of evidence that Marian is a good driver first **quote** the word, phrase or sentence from the story that shows this.

Then **explain in your own words** why the quotation you have chosen shows us that she is a good driver.

Set your answers out in a table like the one below.

| Para | Quotation | Explanation |
|------|-----------|-------------|
| 2 | 'Marian drove the car slowly through the shady suburban streets.' | Lots of children live in the suburbs. By driving slowly Marian will be able to stop if one runs out in to the road. |

As well as being skilled, Marian is very aware of the situation and society she lives in. There are several occasions in the first fifteen paragraphs of the story where Marian knows she is more aware of the situation than Mrs Ericson. Sometimes we can also tell that Mrs Ericson herself realises that Marian knows best.

## Now try this

Read through the story. Each time you find an example of Marian seeming to know best, first **quote** what is written in the story.

Then **explain in your own words** how the quotation that you have chosen shows that Marian knows or understands the situation better than Mrs Ericson does. Make sure you explain what Marian thinks.

Set your answers out in a table like the one below.

| Para | Quotation | Explanation |
|------|-----------|-------------|
| 2 | 'They probably do like it better if a white person shows up with you.' | Marian understands that the problem wasn't caused by Bill talking, but by them both being black. |

Now think about this question. You may want to discuss it with a partner, a group or your class. Try to find as many reasons as possible to build up a really full answer.

- Why does the author work so hard at making Marian seem very able, and much more aware than her employer of what the world is like?

All the things we have looked at so far are part of the writer's **characterisation** of Marian. **Characterisation** just means all the things an author does to create a character and bring that person to life on the page. So far we have seen how Marian is **characterised as** being skilful, aware, and determined.

# Relationships in the story

Another way writers build up and create their characters is by showing what they are like in relation to others. In the story, we see Marian interacting with Mrs Ericson and with the driving inspector.

Have you ever seen one of those cartoons where the person has a little demon on one shoulder and angel on the other? The demon and angel don't talk to each other, just to the person whose shoulders they are sitting on. The demon tries to get the person to do something bad or get into trouble, while the angel tries to keep the person out of trouble and focused on doing good.

In some ways Mrs Ericson and the driving inspector are like the angel and demon. They are there in the story to relate to and influence Marion. We never see them unless they are with her.

## Marian and the driving inspector

When you first read the story you looked for examples of the inspector speaking in what he thinks is a southern accent or dialect, and for examples of him calling Marian by the wrong name.

A lot of this is tied in with the history of slavery in America. From the 1600s onward, thousands of Africans were brought to America against their will to work as slaves. Most of them worked in the southern states, on farms and plantations. Instead of allowing the slaves to use their own African names, their white owners gave them new names, and often chose names for the American-born children of slaves.

Slavery came to an end in the 1860s after the American civil war. This story is set almost a century later. However, by talking to Marian as if she must be from the south, the inspector is showing outdated ideas about the lives of black people in 1950s America. By deciding to call her by a different name, one he chooses, he is trying to take control of her.

## Now try this

Look at this extract from near the start of the story and answer the questions that follow:

> The inspector who finally reached their car was not the stocky one, but a genial, middle-aged man who grunted broadly as he thumbed over their papers. Mrs Ericson started to get out of the car. 'Don't you want to come along?' the inspector asked. 'Mandy and I don't mind company.'
>
> Mrs Ericson was bewildered for a moment. 'No,' she said, and stepped to the curb. 'I might make Marian self-conscious. She's a fine driver, Inspector.'
>
> 'Sure thing,' the inspector said, winking at Mrs Ericson. He slid into the seat beside Marian. 'Turn right at the corner, Mandy-Lou.'

1  Apart from using the wrong name, how else do we see the inspector trying to control Marian?

2  How does Mrs Ericson try to correct the inspector?

The writer does other interesting things with the inspector's speech style too. As well the two features of his speech that we have looked at already, there is also a **contrast** between the way he speaks and the way Marian speaks. The Inspector often speaks in **assumptions** that show his own opinions and prejudices about black people. Marian tends to speak in **facts**.

## Now try this

Tackle these three tasks to help you examine their speech styles.

1  Read through the story. Each time you find an example of the inspector making an assumption, first **quote** what he says. Then **explain in your own words** what he assumes or thinks about Marian. (If you'd like a hint, look for assumptions about Marian's family, sex life, education, intelligence, honesty and background.)

2  Read through the story. **Copy down** each example where Marian speaks to the Inspector using only a fact.

3  **Answer** these questions:

   ■  Why do you think Marian only speaks in facts?

- Is there ever an example of her speaking to him in a different way? Quote it in your answer.

- What happens the only time she speaks in a different way?

The different ways they speak are just part of a whole collection of differences between the inspector and Marian. One you may not have spotted is their education. Marian has a degree, and it's not her fault but her society's fault that she has not been able to use that to get a good job. The inspector is a white man in a racist, sexist society. If he's in the job he's in, he almost certainly doesn't have a degree. Marian must be better educated than he is.

## Now try this

You may want to work with a partner or group to do this. Brainstorm all the ways you can think of that Marian and the inspector are different from each other.

## Marian and Mrs Ericson

Marian is in the car with the inspector for most of the story, but at the start and end we see her with her employer, Mrs Ericson.

## Now try this

Look at this extract from near the start of the story and answer the questions that follow:

> On the afternoon Marian took her second driver's test, Mrs Ericson went with her. 'It's probably better to have someone a little older with you,' Mrs Ericson said as Marian slipped into the driver's seat beside her. 'Perhaps the last time your cousin Bill made you nervous, talking too much on the way.'
>
> 'Yes, Ma'am,' Marian said in her soft unaccented voice. 'They probably do like it better if a white person shows up with you.'

1 The writer calls Marian by her first name but calls Mrs Ericson by her title and surname. What differences between the characters can we see from this?

2 How can you tell from the way the story is written that Mrs Ericson is Marian's employer?

Despite the differences between them, and despite the fact that Marian works for Mrs Ericson, the two women seem to have a close relationship.

## Now try this

Look at the following statements. Copy each one in to your notebook. Beside each statement, note down a quotation from the story to prove the statement. For some of the statements, you should actually be able to find more than one piece of proof.

A. Mrs Ericson thinks Marian deserves to pass her test.

B. Mrs Ericson is able to accept that Marian may know best.

C. Mrs Ericson wants to help Marian stay calm.

D. Mrs Ericson encourages Marian.

E. Mrs Ericson relies on Marian.

F. Mrs Ericson appreciates Marian.

G. The two women are fond of each other.

That all sounds very good, but it doesn't mean the relationship between the two women is perfect.

## Now try this

Read the first section of the story again, up to the point where they arrive at the driving test centre. Look especially at what Marian says. Can you find any suggestion that Marian might think her employer is just slightly taking advantage of her?

## Now try this

Read the following extract from paragraph and answer the questions:

'Oh Marian,' Mrs Ericson exclaimed, 'If only I could pay you half of what you're worth!'

'Now, Mrs Ericson,' Marian said firmly. They looked at each other and smiled with affection.

1   Does Marian think there is any chance of Mrs Ericson giving her a pay rise? How do you know this?

2   List as many reasons as you can think of to explain why Mrs Ericson feels she cannot raise Marian's wages.

## Other language techniques in the story

### Word choice

There are several interesting examples of **word choice** in the story. Of course all words that a writer uses are chosen in some way, but when we talk about **word choice** as a technique we mean that certain words are very carefully and deliberately chosen to obtain particular effects.

There's only one example of explicitly racist word choice in the story. It comes in paragraph 22 when the inspector describes Marian as:

'Old enough to have quite a flock of pickaninnies'

That word *pickaninnies* is a very offensive and racist term for black children.

In fact the inspector's words quoted above are actually even more offensive.

■   How and why does the word *flock* make this statement even more insulting?

When Marian arrives at the driving test centre, we see this passage of description:

Two cars with official insignia on their doors stopped across the street. The inspectors leaped out, very brisk and military in their neat uniforms. Marian's hand tightened on the wheel. 'There's the one who flunked me last time,' she whispered, pointing to a stocky, self-important man who had <u>begun to shout directions</u> at the driver at the head of the line. 'Oh Mrs Ericson.'

## Now try this

Look at the words that have been underlined in the extract above.

1 What kind of word choice would you call this?

2 Why do you think the writer chose to use this sort of word choice to describe what is happening at the driving test centre?

## Literal and figurative language

**Literal language** is language which is actually true. **Figurative language** has a deeper, wider meaning, or helps us to come to a deeper understanding by using comparisons or mental pictures.

For example, we could say that:

**The rocket flew over the moon.**

That's an example of **literal language**. The rocket actually took off from Earth and went so high that it passed above the moon on its way out in to space.

However we could also say that:

**He was over the moon about his new job.**

That doesn't mean he jumped above that crescent-shaped thing that hangs in the sky. It means he felt excited.

## Now try this

Look at the title of the story. Though it seems simple it's actually very clever because it is both literal and figurative.

1 Explain how the title literally fits the story.

2 Explain how the title has a deeper, more figurative meaning too.

## The theme

The **theme** of a story (or of a novel, play, film or poem) is the big idea behind it. The theme is something the writer wants you to think about or learn about. It may be an idea the writer is trying to explore. A theme should be something that you can express using just one or two simple words.

The important theme in this story is **racism**. The driving inspector is determined not to let a black woman pass her driving test, and when she makes one small driving mistake and then snaps at him for commenting on it he takes his chance. He marks four random mistakes on her form and fails her. We also know from the way she describes her first driving test that she has been unfairly failed before

## Now try this

Quite often in the literature exam you will find a question about how a writer handles a certain theme or issue. Working with a partner, a group, or your whole class, decide what the author Angelica Gibb is trying to say to us about racism. What does she want us to realise or understand?

You should try to make your answer as full as possible. You might want to collect your ideas on a spider plan like the one below.

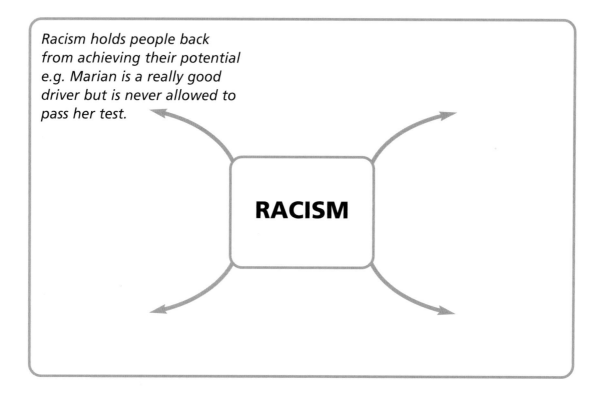

*Racism holds people back from achieving their potential e.g. Marian is a really good driver but is never allowed to pass her test.*

**RACISM**

## Essay writing

Later in this book there is a chapter about how to write a Critical Essay for Intermediate 2. Although the advice in that chapter is general, and will help you to write all your Critical Essays, most of the examples in that chapter are based on 'The Test' and on the work we've done on this story.

You may want to go to that chapter now and work through it to write your first literature essay.

## Possible essay choices

Once you have studied the chapter on essay writing, you might like to try one of the following essays, which are also suitable for 'The Test'.

Above the prose essay choices on the exam paper you will see the following words:

> **Answers to questions in this section should refer to the text and such relevant features as: characterisation, setting, language, key incident(s), structure, climax/turning point, plot, narrative technique, theme, ideas, description . . .**

Now look at the essay choices:

- Choose a novel or a short story in which you feel great sympathy, or intense dislike of, one of the characters.

  Briefly outline the situation in which the character finds himself or herself and show by what means you are made to feel sympathy or dislike.

or

- Choose a prose work of fiction or non-fiction which deals with an important human issue: for example injustice, poverty, or scientific discovery, or religious belief, or any other issue which you regard as important.

  Identify and explain what the issue is and go on to describe the ways in which the writer has made the prose work thought-provoking.

# 4

# Prose: Death of a Spinster

## Getting in

You are about to read a short story. It describes a woman's quiet life and sudden death. Before you read the story, think about the following questions. You should share your answers with a partner, a small group, or your class.

- What sort of job would be a satisfying and interesting one for you? Why do you think you would enjoy this job?

- Imagine yourself at the age of 57. What do you think your life will be like when you are that age?

- If you could choose when, and how, you die, what would you choose?

## Meeting the text

As you read through the story for the first time, make a note of every time the author uses a number:

## Death of a Spinster

1 Each weekday was mapped. When the digital alarm went, she would press the snooze mechanism two separate times so that she would have about ten minutes more in bed. When she got out of bed, she would reset the alarm for next day, making sure each time it was set for a.m. Tomorrow was promised.

2 The day took her to itself like an assembly line. Routine precludes the time to weep. She showered, wearing the floral shower-cap. (She only washed her hair at weekends.) Soaping her body was a sensual ceremony and she always noted how firm she was still in her late fifties, taking a dispassionate inventory of herself like someone viewing an empty house. She dried and dressed in the clothes she had laid out the previous evening.

3   She clicked on the already-filled kettle. She turned on the gas till it clicked alight and put on it the two eggs waiting in their panful of water. She gave the eggs three minutes from the time the water boiled. She toasted one slice of bread and buttered it. She poured the hot water into the cup containing instant coffee and one sweetener. She put one egg, taken out of the pan with a tablespoon and dried with a teacloth, into an eggcup and the other in the saucer beside it. She breakfasted.

4   The dishes were gathered and put in the basin with the remainder of the hot water from the kettle which was then refilled. She always noted how scuffed cheap plastic gets with use. The make-up she applied was a suggestion of who she might be. The timed walk to wait for the bus that was invariably busy brought the brief satisfaction of seeing the tired man with the gentle eyes. He seemed unhappy in a way that made her want to talk to him but she never had.

5   The working day was full of apparent differences that turned out to be the same. She typed letters and dispensed stationery and dealt with problems that didn't really matter. At lunchtime she had a snack alone in the town and looked at some shops and made sure she was back in time to talk for about twenty minutes with Marion Bland. The afternoon was the same as the morning.

6   No matter what shopping she had to do, she was home in time to watch the news on television. The strangeness of the world appalled her but she couldn't resist watching the strangeness. She ate at seven. Lasagne was her favourite. The evening was usually a television programme she had ringed in the Radio Times and TV Times. At nine she had her sherry. Sometimes she had one sherry, sometimes two. Three was an orgy.

7   The evening was also the most dangerous part of her life. Time was less obedient then. Sometimes Margaret and John Hislop came. She didn't always enjoy their visits. They often seemed to be using her as an audience, allowing her to look on at their cosy warmth and predictable banter. But they were the nearest thing to family she had. Sometimes she thought over things that Marion had said and wondered what Marion's life was like. Sometimes she talked aloud to the photo of her nephew, Ronnie Milligan, who was in Canada. Sometimes the fantasies came almost more fierce than she could bear and containing images she could hardly admit. On such nights she took two Mogadon instead of one.

8   These trivia she strung out like charms about the pulse of her life. One day the charms broke. An unscheduled car drove straight in between shopping and talking to Marion. The crowd didn't know her. One man leaning close to her lips heard them give up the meaning of who she had been. In that whisper of breath, that indistinct sound, her life was caught in a moment – politely unheard.

9   Her lightness was loaded into an ambulance. How slim she had stayed. Behind her she was leaving an unpaid gas bill and Marion bereft of about twenty minutes of daily conversation. Her nephew would hear of it later. Margaret and John Hislop would feel bad about having found her so dull. A handsome restaurant waiter she used to give lavish tips would wonder intermittently what had happened to her and his thoughts would be a kind of requiem, duly paid for. The dishes were unwashed. The alarm would be unanswered.

10 Stripping off her prim clothes, they were amazed at the vision they saw. Her body was sensuous in rich underwear. The brassiere and the pants were of pale green, sheer silk, beneath which the dark pubic hair shimmered like Atlantis. They went on with what they had to do, unaware that they had witnessed the stubborn resplendence of unfulfilled dreams.

**William McIlvanney**

 **Thinking through**

First, share your answers to the 'Meeting the Text' task you were given at the start of the story. Then work out the answers to the following tasks and questions:

1   Why do you think the writer uses so many numbers throughout the story? What is he trying to say about the woman's life?

2   List all the other people mentioned in the story, apart from the main character.

3   Now put these characters in order of how well you think they actually know the woman. Put the person you think knows her best at the top of the list, with the one who you think knows her least well at the bottom.

## Let's get to work

As we study this story we'll see how William McIlvanney builds up a complete picture of the woman and her narrow life. We'll see how her life is governed by routine and will explore her loneliness. We will find out about her fear of risks, and the chances she misses because of this.

## The main character's narrow life

### A daily routine

The woman in this story lives her life to a rigid timetable. Every weekday follows the same pattern.

### Now try this

See if you can list the woman's daily routine by following details in the story. The first few items have been done for you. Don't forget her lunchtime and evening routines.

| | |
|---|---|
| *7 a.m.* | *Alarm rings. Press snooze* |
| *7.05* | *Alarm rings again. Snooze again* |
| *7.10* | *Get up* |

Since none of this sounds very exciting or varied, you might wonder why she has allowed her life to get into this rut. The answer comes in paragraph 2 when the writer tells us:

**Routine precludes the time to weep.**

That words 'precludes' means cuts out, or prevents. This woman is tremendously sad and lonely. If she follows a routine, and keeps herself busy, she will not have time to stop and cry about the state her life is in, or the relationships she wants and does not have, or the things she is missing out on.

It follows on from this that the times which are least controlled by her routine are very hard for the main character. Paragraph 7 tells us:

> **The evening was also the most dangerous part of her life**

The word 'dangerous' seems almost out of place. It's an example of **emotive language**, strong language that tries to stir up the reader's emotions.

■ Why are evenings *'dangerous'* for this woman?

## A lack of money

Something else that restricts this woman's life is that her job is not well paid, and she is not well off. There are lots of clues in the story that suggest this.

### Now try this

Read the following quotations. Write each one in your notebook, and beside it write a sentence or two to explain how this tells you that the woman has little money to spare.

1  'how scuffed cheap plastic gets with use' (para 4)

2  'to wait for the bus that was invariably late' (para 4)

3  'at lunchtime she had a snack' (para 5)

4  'and looked at some shops' (para 5)

5  'what shopping she had to do' (para 6)

6  ' an unpaid gas bill' (para 9)

7  'lavish tips' (para 9)

Now look back again at paragraph 2. We are told the woman is:

> **in her late fifties**

This means that she will probably have to retire in just a few years. She won't be going to work each day any more.

## Now try this

Explain in detail two reasons why her retirement in just a few years time will make her life more difficult. Use the starter below.

*The writer tells us the woman is 'in her late fifties' which means she is not far off retirement. This will make her life harder and sadder for two reasons. Firstly . . . Secondly . . .*

### A dull job

As well as a rigid routine, and a restrictive lack of money, this woman also has a boring job.

## Now try this

Read paragraph 5 and answer the following questions:

1   Which two separate sentences tell us her job is boring? Quote each one.

2   Which expression tells us that much of her work is pointless?

3   Which word tells us that her friend at work, Marion, is boring? How does this word reveal this to us?

### Fear of risks

So, if the woman's job is boring, and also not very well paid, we might wonder why she does not leave. It might be because of her age – the older you are, the harder it is to persuade someone to give you a new job. It probably isn't because of her skills and abilities. If she does her work as efficiently as she runs her life, then she's probably very good at it. The problems she deals with each day may not really matter, but the colleagues she solves them for probably appreciate her effectiveness.

It seems most likely that she does not look for another job because she is afraid of the risk of rejection. She is just too scared to try. This is only one of several risks in the story that she seems afraid to take.

## Now try this

Read paragraphs 4 and 9 again. For each paragraph, explain what the risk is that she does not take.

## Unfulfilling relationships

This leads us on to yet another aspect of this woman's rather restricted life. The relationships she does have, such as they are, seem rather unfulfilling.

We've already seen from Marion's surname, Bland, that she must be a rather dull person to talk to.

- How can we tell from paragraph 7 that, despite their daily chats, she really does not know Marion very well?
- How can we tell from paragraph 9 that Marion never really felt very close to her?

We are told in paragraph 7 that our central character has

**a nephew, Ronnie Milligan, who lived in Canada.**

If she has a nephew, she must have, or must have had, a brother or sister who is Ronnie's mother or father. There's no mention of that sibling in her story.

- What do you think might have happened to the woman's sister or brother? Try to think of at least three different explanations for why we don't find any mention of this person in the story.
- Why do you think she talks to the photo of her nephew?
- Why do you think she doesn't phone him, or write to him, instead of just talking to the photo?

The woman has two friends, Margaret and John Hislop, who are mentioned in paragraph 7 as sometimes coming to visit her.

- How does she feel about their visits?
- Bearing in mind your answer to the question above, why do you think she keeps inviting them over?
- One sentence in this section about the Hislops is meant to make you feel very sad as you read it. Quote the sentence.
- How do the Hislops feel about her after her death?

When we see what this woman's life is like, we can find lots of reasons to feel sympathy for her. However, when we remember that it is partly her fault her life has ended up that way, we may find her rather frustrating.

## Now try this

Draw a line down the centre of your page and use the two headings shown below. Down the left side, think of as many reasons as you can for why you sympathise with or feel sorry for the woman. On the right, list all the things you think she does wrong, or those things that frustrate you about her. You may wish to discuss this with a group or partner.

| Reasons to feel sympathy | Reasons to find her frustrating |
|---|---|
| Her friends make her feel uncomfortable | She never talks to the man at the bus stop |

# A hint of something else

So far we have a picture of a woman who has allowed her life to become sad and boring. However, that doesn't mean that is the way she wants it to be.

In paragraph 2 we find the following words:

> **Soaping her body was a sensual ceremony and she always noted how firm she was still in her late fifties**

The word *sensual* is very important here. It suggests physical pleasure, even something sexual. The woman is very proud of her body, which is still slim and firm.

- At what other point in the story are we reminded of her slimness?

Now skip ahead in the story and read paragraph 7.

- Copy out the sentence from that paragraph which alludes to her having sexual thoughts.

- Which word used in paragraph 6 prepared us for the idea of something sexual?

The ending of the story is very important in telling us that the woman never gave up hope of having a lover, a partner or a husband. When the undertakers are preparing her body for burial they find something the writer calls 'a vision'.

> **Her body was sensuous in rich underwear.**

This is a strong contrast with the 'prim' outer clothes she is wearing. Even though nobody knows, or sees, she dresses every day in beautiful underwear, underwear that is probably very expensive for someone on a tight budget. She dresses every day as if today is the day when she won't end up alone. The writer describes this as

**the stubborn resplendence of unfulfilled dreams**

■ Explain, in your own words, what these last few words of the story mean.

We'll find one more hint of something else in her life later in this chapter when we examine the Atlantis image from the end of the story.

## Imagery

Most of this story is written in quite plain and simple prose. However, towards the end McIlvanney uses two very striking **images**, or word pictures.

The first is in paragraph 8, just after he has finished describing her life and routine.

**These trivia she strung out like charms about the pulse of her life. One day the charms broke.**

This image is actually quite a complex **metaphor**. You should know that a metaphor is a comparison in which one thing is said to be another thing. For example, if someone commentating on a rugby match says

**That player is an animal**

it doesn't mean the player is hairy, with a tail, and has paws instead of feet. It means he plays in a rough, violent, animal-like way.

Similarly if we describe a musician as

**a wizard on the piano**

it doesn't mean that she stands over it waving a magic wand and making sounds come out. It means that she is highly skilled, and creates musical effects that seem almost impossible or magical.

In the image from paragraph 7, the separate details are all individual little metaphors.

# Literal/non-literal

Words can be used in a **literal** and a **non-literal** sense. When a word is taken literally it means exactly what it says, for example, 'The knife edge was very sharp.' Sharp, here, means a cutting edge. If we said, 'The professor has a very sharp mind', we would be using a non-literal meaning for sharp - i.e. that the professor was very clever. The literal meaning would be that the professor's brain had a physical edge to it!

## Now try this

Explain what each detail of the image means or suggests. Use the format below:

*The charms stand for . . .*

*The pulse in her wrist stands for . . .*

*The breaking of the bracelet stands for . . .*

The second striking image is in paragraph 10:

> **Her body was sensuous in rich underwear. The brassiere and the pants were of pale green, sheer silk, beneath which the dark pubic hair shimmered like Atlantis.**

This image is a little bit trickier to pin down. To understand it you need to know about the legend of Atlantis.

The legend says that there used to be an amazing island kingdom called Atlantis. It prospered for many years, until eventually it was consumed by storms and flooding and sank beneath the waves, never to be seen again.

So far so good. We can accept that Atlantis is a kingdom that disappeared never to be seen again. Now let's look at the two possible explanations what McIlvanney might be saying about the woman by using the Atlantis image.

**He could be saying:**

Just as the legend says Atlantis once existed, so McIlvanney is saying that the woman's sexual or romantic life (represented by the pubic hair seen beneath her beautiful underwear) did exist once. In her past, she did have a more romantic, more exciting life.

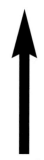

**If you accept this explanation you are more convinced by what the legend says**

**Or he could be saying:**

Atlantis is a legend, a story. It never actually existed. The woman's sexual or romantic life (represented by the pubic hair seen beneath her beautiful underwear) also never existed. It was just a fantasy, imagined and wanted by her but never true.

**If you accept this explanation you are more convinced by the fact that *the story of Atlantis is only a legend***

## Now try this

First of all, decide which interpretation of the image you accept as being the right one. Next, write a paragraph in your notebook, using your own words, to explain what the Atlantis image means. Then, pair up with someone who disagrees with you and has chosen the other interpretation. Try to persuade that person to agree with you by defending your point of view. Then let the other person try to persuade you to agree with them.

## Unusual choices

McIlvanney makes some rather unusual choices in this story. He does things most writers don't do.

Firstly, he never gives his main character a name. He just refers to her as 'she'. This isn't because he forgot to name her. It isn't because he couldn't think of a name. There's a reason why she has no name.

■ Why do you think McIlvanney does not give the woman a name? What is he trying to say about her?

His second unusual choice comes even before the story begins. He gives it a title, 'Death of a Spinster', which seems to give away how the story ends. Most writers would want the woman's death at the end of the story to be a surprise for the reader.

The reason the story is called 'Death of a Spinster' is because the writer wants to explore a deeper meaning. He is not just telling us that the woman will **literally** be dead and gone by the end of the story. The title has a **metaphorical** meaning, a deeper and more thoughtful meaning, too.

■ What is the metaphorical meaning of the story's title?

## Now try this

Write a pair of paragraphs in your notebook to explain clearly what the unusual choices are that McIlvanney makes, and why he makes them.

The title is interesting for another reason too. McIlvanney uses very careful word choice when he describes the woman as

**a spinster**

## Now try this

Look up the word 'spinster' in a dictionary and write down its meaning. Now write down the word which describes a man in the same position.

This word 'spinster' actually has quite **negative connotations**. You wouldn't use it to describe a woman in her twenties. You wouldn't use it to describe a woman who lived with her partner. You wouldn't use it to describe someone who's playing the field, and going out with lots of different men rather than settling down with one. Instead it implies a woman who is single because nobody really wanted her, someone who's been left on the shelf, someone who'll never get married because nobody will ever feel like marrying her.

Now look again at the word you decided was the male equivalent of spinster. You probably wrote 'bachelor'. Interestingly, that word has none of the same negative connotations. In fact it suggests almost the opposite – someone who's having fun and avoiding being tied down.

## Theme

One theme of this story would be loneliness.

### Now try this

Work with a partner, your group, or the class, to decide on another theme that you think McIlvanney is also exploring in this story.

Put each of your two themes in the centre of a piece of paper. Around the theme, build up details and quotations from the story, creating a spider plan to prove that the themes are being explored.

You may wish to present your spider plan to the class as a poster, overhead or PowerPoint.

### Now try this

To show how well you know the story, you are going to write a paragraph that could fit into it. You should try to copy McIlvanney's style as closely as possible. The paragraph you write should be able to slip into the story between paragraphs 7 and 8. Describe the woman packing her bag in the evening, so that she will have everything in there, ready to take to work the next morning. Think about how well prepared she always is, and the kind of items she would pack.

## Possible essay choices

Once you have studied the chapter on essay writing, you might like to try one of the essays below, which are all suitable for 'Death of a Spinster'.

Above the prose essay choices on the exam paper you will see the following words:

Answers to questions in this section should refer to the text and such relevant features as: characterisation, setting, language, key incident(s), structure, climax/turning point, plot, narrative technique, theme, ideas, description . . .

Now look at the essay choices:

- Choose a character from a novel or a short story who seems to you to be unfortunate in life, or for whom the ending of the story is unhappy.

  Show how much of the character's misfortune you feel is caused by his or her own personality, and how much by other circumstances in the short story or novel.

or

- Choose a novel or a short story in which there is an obvious climax or turning point.

  Show how the writer leads up to this turning point or climax, and say what is its significance for the rest of the story.

or

- A short story often ends in a surprising but satisfying way.

  Concentrating on the ending of a story, explain the success of the ending for you.

or

- Choose a novel or a short story in which you feel great sympathy for, or intense dislike of, one of the characters.

  Briefly outline the situation in which the character finds himself or herself and show by what means you are made to feel sympathy or dislike.

# 5

# Prose: If I Quench Thee

## Getting in

You are about to read a short story. It begins with an argument between a father and daughter but soon turns into something far more serious. Before you read the story, think about the following questions. You should share your answers with a partner, a small group, or your class.

- What was the last thing you argued with one of your parents about? How did the argument end?

- Is there something you believe in strongly that your parents don't agree with? What is it?

- What kind of person do you think your parents would like you to marry one day? Is this like or unlike the kind of life partner you would choose for yourself?

## Meeting the text

This story is told from the point of view of a man called Arthur Stern. We hear what he hears and see what he sees. We know what he knows. We overhear his thoughts and memories. Although Stern does not narrate the story, it concentrates on him and we never leave his side.

As you read through the story for the first time, you are going to make two lists of details from it:

1   The story contains a violent crime:

- What is the crime?

- Who is the criminal?

- Who is the victim?

- Where does the crime occur?

- What is the criminal's motive?

- How is the crime committed?

2   Stern can be very negative and critical. Every time you catch him
    having a critical thought, or expressing a critical opinion, write it
    down. Again, note the paragraph number for each detail. (It might
    help you to know that Stern is critical of his daughter's flat; about
    her; about the area of New York she lives in; and about her
    neighbours.)

## If I Quench Thee

1   Arthur Stern looked past his denim-clad daughter at the apartment she had taken in one of
    Manhattan's ghettos. It was the first time he had seen it and he frowned critically. A rickety
    wicker settee served as a couch. The top of an ancient and probably unworkable combination
    TV-radio cabinet was used as a bar, and held two bottles of cheap rye. The lifelike poster of
    Communist rebel Che Guevara that decorated the otherwise plain wall behind the bar
    deepened the hue of Stern's pink complexion. Closing the door behind him, he handed her
    his coat and said, 'For God's sake, Monica, put on a bra. There's not much to that blouse
    you're wearing.'

2   Monica stood on her toes and kissed his cheek. 'Don't be so old-fashioned. If God wanted
    these things bound, I would have been born with a Playtex living –'

**3** 'Damn it! That isn't funny!'

**4** 'OK! OK!' Raising her hands like a holdup victim, Monica retreated backward through the beaded curtains to her bedroom. She shouted from inside, 'Hey I'm glad you came to visit, Dad.'

**5** 'Thought I'd surprise you since you never visit me.'

**6** 'I was going to get in touch with you –'

**7** 'I'll bet.'

**8** 'I was. I've got a surprise of my own.'

**9** 'Nothing you might say or do would surprise me any more.'

**10** Monica returned, mixed two highballs, and sat on the settee next to Stern. They clinked glasses. He said, 'Happy birthday.'

**11** 'Whoa. I'm not twenty-four until next week. Don't rush it.'

**12** 'I didn't know what to give you as a present Monica, so I thought I'd find out what you needed and write a cheque.'

**13** 'Well I don't really *need* anything –'

**14** 'Seems to me you could use everything.'

**15** 'Like what? I have my home, my job –'

**16** 'Some home.'

**17** 'The location's convenient for work.'

**18** 'Toiling for peanuts among a bunch of savages –'

**19** 'Daddy – please! I do social work because I have a conscience.'

**20** 'What kind of conscience prods a daughter to leave her own flesh and blood for a band of slum dwellers?'

**21** 'You don't need me. These people do.'

**22** 'Need you? Do you think your mother – God rest her soul – and I slaved to build that mink farm upstate just for ourselves?'

**23** When Monica failed to answer, Stern continued, 'We did it to get you away from the city – the slums – and the kind of people who dwell in them.'

**24** 'These *kind* of people are good people, dad. All they need is some help –'

**25** 'Bull! All they need is to get off their butts and help themselves like I did.'

**26** Monica gulped her drink, took a deep breath and said, 'You've always been strong, Dad. That's why you can't understand people who are weak.'

27  The shrill buzz of the doorbell interrupted them, and Monica looked a little uncomfortable. Stern said, 'Expecting company?'

28  'No. Not really.' She fumbled with the buttons on her blouse. 'It – well – it might be Tod Humbert.'

29  'Another social worker?'

30  'Much more than that.'

31  A second, more insistent buzz made Stern wince.

32  'Buzz him back, will you?'

33  The sound of a man coming upstairs was followed by a vigorous tapping on the door. Monica opened it and said, 'Oh – hi, Tod –'

34  A tall, thin black man wearing a short leather jacket and blue jeans wrapped his arms around her waist, kissed her on both cheeks and said, 'You're looking bad, baby. Superbad!'

35  Monica gently withdrew from his embrace and turned sheepishly towards her father.

36  'Tod – I – I – want you to meet Arthur Stern, my father.'

37  A bright smile flashed across the black man's face. He walked forward, hand extended and said, 'Mr Stern, this is a pleasure, sir.'

38  Ignoring Tod completely, Stern rose. 'Monica, my coat please.'

39  The girl looked pleadingly at him, then went wordlessly into the bedroom. Tod sat down on the settee and stared silently at his outstretched legs and crossed ankles. Stern wrote out a cheque and handed it to Monica when she returned with his coat.

40  'Fill in whatever you need.'

41  'May I borrow your pen?'

42  'Of course. Here.'

43  Monica blinked steadily as she filled out the cheque and handed it back to him. The amount read: *Nothing!*

*   *   *   *

44  The odour of rancid food that pervaded the hall disappeared as Stern stepped into the cold night air. He crumpled the rejected cheque in his fist, threw it into the gutter and ordered

himself to be calm. However, his stomach churned and his temples throbbed as he envisioned the black man with his daughter, the black man's arms around Monica . . .

**45** Stern strode around the block, trying to decide what to do. He could disown Monica and wash his hands of all responsibility towards her. But the very thought made him shudder. He could go home and hope time would heal the wounds. But what if that failed? Finally he decided he could return to her apartment, make apologies and an effort to tolerate Humbert, and start rebuilding the damaged relationship.

**46** Choice number three was most logical, of course, so Stern swallowed his pride and marched back to his daughter's building. An elderly man who was leaving held the inner door open as Stern entered, making it unnecessary for him to ring the bell. A shaft of yellow light slanting from the recessed hall at the top of the stairs indicated a partially opened apartment door. The sound of familiar voices made him hesitate at the foot of the landing. He heard Tod Humbert say, 'Don't feel bad, honey. It's good to be snubbed occasionally. Humbles the ego.'

**47** 'Thanks for being so understanding Tod.'

**48** 'You're extra special. Marrying you will be the greatest thrill of my life.'

**49** A sudden upsurge of blood pressure made Stern grip the bannister rail for support. He had visions of friends and business associates sporting lewd grins and knowing leers. Damn it! He could stand her seeing Humbert, but not this – not marriage, a black son-in-law.

**50** Fists clenched, teeth grating, he left the building again and ducked into the doorway of an abandoned house, diagonally across the street. The building hatred he was feeling now conjured up remembrances a quarter-century old. His mind filled with reflections of Korea, of another people, different in skin colour, an alien race that had threatened him and his fellow commandoes. A threat he had eliminated with bullets, piano wire, and bare hands.

**51** Once again, after twenty-five years, he felt threatened. But this type of threat was different, wasn't it? New York wasn't a jungle – or was it? You couldn't react here the way you could in Korea – or could you . . .?

**52** If the sight of Tod Humbert emerging several minutes later from Monica's hallway stimulated Stern's adrenal glands, he showed no sign of it. He remained still until the black man disappeared around the corner, then he followed. After walking a deserted block, he called out, 'Mr Humbert!' Tod Humbert glanced warily over his shoulder. 'It's me, Arthur Stern.'

**53** Stern broke into a trot to catch up, then feigned breathlessness. He said, 'I hope you can forgive my rude behaviour. Monica and I had angry words before you arrived and I let my emotions get the best of me. I was just returning to apologise when I happened to see you.'

**54** The black man chuckled, extended his hand and said, 'We all have our faults, don't –'

**55** He never finished his sentence. Stern gripped his outstretched hand, jerked him forward and kneed him in the groin. As Tod's legs buckled, he clawed wildly. Stern felt a burning sensation on one side of his face and heard cloth tear. Both men collapsed against a row of foul-smelling garbage cans lined up before a run-down tenement. The clatter of metal and the screech of an exasperated cat shattered the night. Stern crawled on top of Humbert, gripped his hair with both hands and pounded his head against the sidewalk. An edge-of-the-hand chop across the black man's throat ended the conflict.

56 Stern lumbered to his feet, glanced about, then twisted his tie and tore his shirt. The facial cut he had received before falling bled enough to satisfy him. He knew that muggings occurred with startling regularity in this section of New York City. He imagined how Monica would feel when her own father was victimised. It would be The Lesson that would teach her to despise the ghetto dwellers for the depths to which most of them sunk, and bring her home again to her own kind. Especially when he proved his attacker was Tod Humbert!

57 Yellow squares of light began flashing in various tenements, and somewhere nearby a window rattled open. Stern clutched his wounded face with one hand and staggered in to the gutter shouting for the police.

\* \* \* \*

58 Arthur Stern gestured in disbelief as he spoke to the bored, flat-faced detective sitting across the desk from him. 'As I told the patrolman, I was just walking along when this man attacked me. I came back to the neighbourhood because I wanted to talk to my daughter again. You can imagine my shock – my horror – when the mugger turned out to be the man my daughter had introduced me to only an hour earlier. The man – my God – the man she was going to marry.'

59 A detective put his head through the door. 'His daughter's here.'

60 'Send her in.'

61 Monica, complexion drained, entered listlessly. Stern went to her, and gently squeezed her shoulders, saying, 'Thanks for coming, baby.'

62 She stood stiffly, not returning his embrace. Instead, she said coldly, 'I thought they handcuffed murderers.'

63 Stern felt a sudden chill on his back. He clutched her harder. 'It was self-defence,' he said. 'Humbert tried to mug me.'

64 'Tod could never raise his hand in violence to anyone. It would be against his principles, his way of life. If there was violence, *you* caused it. And I'll tell that to a jury. You murdered someone very dear to me.'

65 'It isn't murder when . . . someone like that . . .' Stern looked at the flat-faced detective, who was watching him closely. Then he shook his head, hissed air through clenched teeth and said, 'Damn it, how could you even *think* of marrying him, Monica!'

66 'Marry him? What are you talking about?'

67 'Don't pretend! I came back to apologise tonight and overheard your conversation from the hall. He said marrying you would be the greatest thrill of his life.'

68 Monica stared at him for a long moment. Then she shrugged his hands from her shoulders,

fumbled through her purse and produced a snapshot of a blond man in an army medical uniform. 'This is the surprise I had for you, Dad. Next month, when he gets discharged, I'm going to marry *this* man.'

69 Stern's eyes grew wide as they rested on the picture. He tried to speak but his voice failed him. For the first time in his life, Arthur Stern knew fear as Monica's tear-stained face moved from side to side and he heard her say, 'Tod was going to marry me, all right. He – was an ordained minister . . .'

**William E. Chambers**

## Thinking through

First, share your answers to the 'Meeting the Text' questions you were given at the start of the story.

The story ends in a **twist**, an event which surprises the reader and is a huge shock for Stern. Work out the answers to the following five questions:

1    What is the shock for Stern?

2    What mistaken idea did Stern have? Which sentence in paragraph 48 was important in him developing that idea?

3    What did that sentence in paragraph 48 really mean?

4    Explain how the writer managed to get this twist to be a shock for the reader, as well as for Stern.

5    Look at the description of Monica's fiancé at the end of the story. Ironically, she's engaged to just the sort of man her father would like her to get married to. Find at least three reasons why her fiancé would get her father's approval.

## Let's get to work

As we study this story we are going to look mainly at the three characters in it. We'll look at the relationships between them, and our response as readers to those characters. We'll start, as the story does, with Stern's relationship with his daughter Monica.

## Stern and Monica

We've already looked at Stern's very critical attitude. Monica and her lifestyle are often targets of this criticism. It's clear that we are looking at a relationship that has been bad for some time.

■ How can we tell from the first five paragraphs of the story that Stern and his daughter do not get on well, and are not close?

The first part of the story, when they are in Monica's flat, probably covers only about ten minutes of their lives. Yet in that time we see a number of ways in which they treat each other badly.

### Now try this

Read paragraphs 1 to 43 again. Then copy and complete the PEE grid below.

| POINT about a character | EVIDENCE quoted from the story | EXPLANATION in your own words |
|---|---|---|
| Stern is instantly critical of his daughter | 'For God's sake Monica, put on a bra.' | The very first thing he says is critical – he doesn't even try to start their time together nicely. |
| Monica is capable of trying to be friendly towards him. | | |
| Monica knows exactly how to wind her father up. | | |
| Stern is bitter about the way his daughter treats him. | | |
| Stern can be sarcastic towards Monica. | | |
| Stern is capable of trying to be nice to Monica. | | |
| Stern doesn't actually know his daughter very well. | | |

*continued*

| POINT about a character | EVIDENCE quoted from the story | EXPLANATION in your own words |
|---|---|---|
| Stern attacks the things that matter to Monica. | | |
| Stern is protective of his daughter. | | |
| Monica uses silence to punish her father. | | |
| Monica rejects what her father offers her. | | |

The two characters have very different ways of life. Despite being father and daughter, they have different lifestyles, values and beliefs.

## Now try this

Copy and complete the spine and rib plan to display the contrasts.

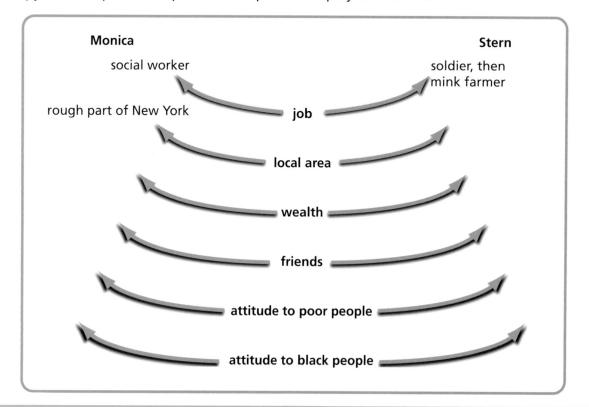

Monica — Stern

social worker — soldier, then mink farmer

rough part of New York — job

— local area

— wealth

— friends

— attitude to poor people

— attitude to black people

One particular contrast between them is what they do to make a living. Monica is a social worker in a tough part of New York; her father, a former soldier, now owns a mink farm.

The author did not choose these jobs by accident. Each job says something about the person who does it.

## Now try this

Answer these questions:

1 Monica is a social worker. What is this supposed to say to us about her character and personality?

2 Stern used to be a soldier, and clearly felt that this was an important job and one he was suited to. What is this supposed to say to us about his character and personality?

3 Stern made his money by setting up and running a mink farm. What is this supposed to say to us about his character and personality? It might help you if you consider how different a person he would be if the author had decided to make him a farmer of free range, organic eggs instead.

Stern's relationship with Monica is not completely dreadful. Although he commits a terrible crime, he does do so out of a twisted kind of love for his daughter. Also, at one point in the story, we do see him nearly choosing to do the right thing and 'rebuild the damaged relationship'.

## Now try this

Read paragraph 45 again. Stern comes up with three possible plans.

1 Explain each plan in your own words.

2 Which plan does he choose?

3 Why is this the best one?

4 Why would the other two plans both seem the same from Monica's point of view?

Stern thinks of his chosen plan as 'the most logical of course'. It's ironic that, when he goes back to carry out this logical plan, he ends up committing a murder based on totally false logic and a wrong idea.

Looking at the father–daughter relationship has allowed us to find out quite a lot about Monica as well as Stern. Since Stern is the main character, let's now look at him in more detail.

## Stern

The first thing to say about Stern is that his name matters. Though we know his first name, Arthur, the author almost always refers to him by his surname.

- Look up the word 'stern' in a dictionary. What does it mean?

- Why do you think the author chose that word for this character's name? What does it tell us about his personality?

### Creating a point of view

The whole story is told from Stern's point of view. Although Stern does not narrate the story, it concentrates on him, and we never leave his side. Even when Stern is alone, we follow him and know what he is up to.

## Now try this

To see how the writer has established this point of view, look for the following and record them in your notebook. Try to find as many examples as you can for each one.

- Things Stern remembers

- Things Stern does when there is no one there to do see him do them

- Things Stern imagines

- Things Stern thinks, but never says out loud

One huge element of Stern's view of life is his hatred of black people. He never makes any effort to talk to Tod or get to know him. Tod's skin colour is the only thing Stern can see.

## Now try this

Skim read the story again, starting from paragraph 34. Count up how many times Tod is described as a 'black man'.

### Stern's physical reactions

Stern's emotions and thoughts are very tied in to his body, and his physical reactions. That's probably why it's so easy for his racist thoughts to lead on to a physically violent murder. All the way through the story we see him, or his body, reacting to outside stimuli.

## Now try this

Go through the story, looking at the following paragraphs.

1, 31, 44, 45, 49, 50, 52, 63, 65, 69

As you read, make a table like the one below. On one side write down what the stimulus is. On the other, quote Stern's physical reaction.

| Stimulus | Reaction |
|----------|----------|
| Stern looks at Monica's flat | 'he frowned critically' p1 |

### Stern's past

We have already seen how Stern's current career as a mink farmer reveals something about his personality. Let's now look at his earlier, military career which he remembers in paragraph 50:

> The building hatred he was feeling now conjured up remembrances a quarter-century old. His mind filled with reflections of Korea, of another people, different in skin colour, an alien race that had threatened him and his fellow commandoes. A threat he had eliminated with bullets, piano wire, and bare hands.

The mention of Korea tells us that Stern was a soldier in the US army, and fought in the Korean war in the mid 1950s.

## Now try this

1  What does this whole extract tell us about Stern's attitude to people he thinks of as foreign or different?

2  Look at the word 'alien'. What does that particular word tell us about his attitude to people he thinks of as foreign or different?

We are told he used 'bullets, piano wire, and bare hands' to fight off the Koreans. We would expect a soldier to use bullets. The mention of 'bare hands' is a bit more worrying. It suggests he was prepared to get into fights that were very close and personal.

The mention of 'piano wire' is even more of a worry. This weapon would be used to kill someone. Stern would have sneaked up behind an unsuspecting enemy, wrapped the piano wire around the person's throat, and pulled it tight to strangle them. The enemy would not know Stern was coming and not have a chance to fight back. In other words, Stern has gone beyond the actions a soldier should carry out in a fair war. He has murdered before.

## Jumping to conclusions

At a crucial point in the story, Stern gets the idea that his daughter Monica is going to marry Tod Humbert.

> ⚠️ **It's important not to blame Stern for the conclusion he jumps to**. He has lots of evidence leading him to his assumption. In fact there is so much evidence that what he thinks seems quite reasonable. However **we should blame him for what he *does***. His actions are totally wrong, and are carried out in cold blood, with planning.

Having said that, let's look at the evidence Stern bases his assumption on.

## Now try this

Read through the story from paragraph 1 to paragraph 48. Whenever you find a piece of evidence which makes Stern think what he does, quote it. Then in your own words write a sentence or two to explain why this helps Stern to think what he does.

Once Stern has jumped to his conclusion, he starts planning how to prevent such a wedding from happening.

## Stern's plan

If you look at paragraph 51 you will see Stern asking himself a series of **rhetorical questions**.

■ What does the last question suggest?

By the time paragraph 52 begins, Stern has come up with his plan. It's extremely clever. He totally wins Tod's trust, then exploits that weakness to draw Tod into an unexpected fight that such a gentle person cannot win. Finally, Stern makes sure that he gets the police involved so he can tell his (totally made up) side of the story.

## Now try this

Read paragraphs 52 to 56 again. Tell the story of the crime by creating a cartoon strip to show what happens step by step. Put the words the characters say in speech bubbles.

Then answer the following questions:

1 Why does Stern call Tod '*Mr Humbert*' in paragraph 52?

2 Why does Stern '*feign breathlessness*' in paragraph 53?

3 Why does Stern '*glance about*' in paragraph 56?

4 Why does Stern twist his tie and tear his shirt in paragraph 56?

5 Why does Stern want to get the police involved? (After all, if no one has seen the crime, he could just leave Tod's body there and make the death seem like a random attack in a tough part of the city.)

However, Stern's pan unravels. Look at this extract from paragraph 58:

> I was just walking along when this man attacked me. I came back to the neighbourhood because I wanted to talk to my daughter again. You can imagine my shock – my horror – when the mugger turned out to be the man my daughter had introduced me to only an hour earlier. The man – my God – the man she was going to marry.

This is Stern's planned lie. It's what he wants the police to believe.

## Now try this

Read on in the story from this point. When you find the thing that Stern says which shows that his remarks in paragraph 58 were a lie, write it down.

So, Stern is not so clever after all.

### Tod

We only find out the whole truth about Tod at the end of the story, when we learn he was a church minister. This is a part of the twist, and it surprises us nearly as much as it surprises Stern.

## Now try this

Divide a piece of paper into two columns. On one side, put down all the details you can think of that describe what you think a typical church minister would be like. You might want to think about age, clothing, behaviour, the way this person would speak, and the kind of setting you find that person in. On the other side of the paper, list what the story tells us about Tod. You might want to work with a partner or group for this task.

Tod can at first seem like a perfect person. He's a man of God, he works among disadvantaged people, and he seems to treat everyone he meets with respect and warmth. Sadly, some of his good qualities become dangerous to him. He never sees anyone's bad side, so he never sees how dangerous Stern is. He's too innocent for his own good.

## Now try this

Copy and complete the diagram below with details from the story. You can use either quotations, or short explanations of events that happen in the story.

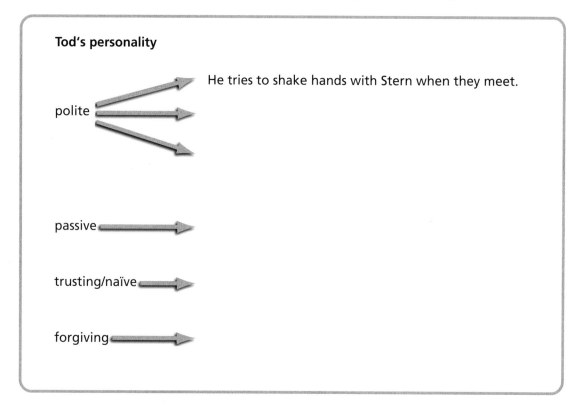

**Tod's personality**

polite → He tries to shake hands with Stern when they meet.

passive →

trusting/naïve →

forgiving →

> ### Now try this
>
> If you could tell Tod to do something different at any particular point in the story, what would you want him to do and at what point in the story would you want him to do it?

## Monica

Monica makes some big mistakes in this story. She begins to plan the seeds of an idea in Stern's mind. This idea eventually leads him to murder Tod.

> ### Now try this
>
> Read paragraphs 8, 30 and 34. Write a paragraph to explain what Monica says and does to start giving Stern the wrong idea.

What Monica does not say or do causes just as much trouble as the things she does say and do. In paragraph 36 she says:

> **'Tod – I – I – want you to meet Arthur Stern, my father.'**

It's a nice polite introduction. However, she doesn't introduce Tod to her father.

■ What should she have said about Tod? How could this have prevented trouble later?

Monica's next mistake comes after her father ignores Tod and says that he's leaving. She gets his coat and lets him go.

■ What should she have said at this point in the story? How could this have prevented trouble later?

This doesn't mean that Monica is a bad person. She has many good qualities.

## Now try this

Copy and complete the two think bubbles to show the two sides of Monica.

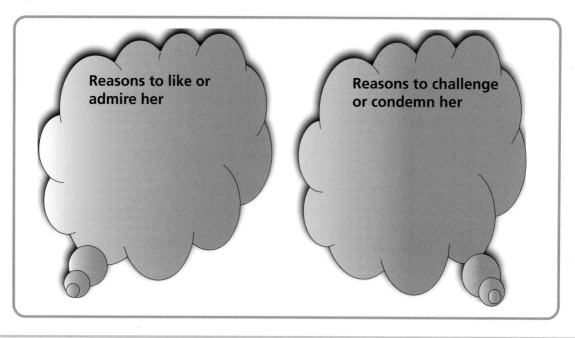

**Reasons to like or admire her**

**Reasons to challenge or condemn her**

## Possible essay tasks

Now that you've finished studying this story, you could tackle the following essay questions. Remember to follow the advice from the chapter about how to write literature essays.

Above the prose essay choices on the exam paper you will see the following words:

> **Answers to questions in this section should refer to the text and such relevant features as: characterisation, setting, language, key incident(s), structure, climax/turning point, plot, narrative technique, theme, ideas, description . . .**

Now look at the essay choices:

- Choose a novel or a short story in which there is an obvious climax or turning point.

  Show how the writer leads up to this turning point or climax, and say what is its significance for the rest of the story.

  or

■ A short story often ends in a surprising but satisfying way.

Concentrating on the ending of a story, explain the success of the ending for you.

or

■ Choose a novel or a short story in which you feel great sympathy for, or intense dislike of, one of the characters.

Briefly outline the situation in which the character finds himself for herself and show by what means you are made to feel sympathy or dislike.

or

■ Choose a prose work of fiction or non-fiction which deals with an important human issue: for example injustice, or poverty, or scientific discovery, or religious belief, or any other issue which you regard as important.

Identify and explain what the issue is and go on to describe the ways in which the writer has made the prose work thought provoking.

# 6

# Poetry: Local Colour

## Getting in

Before you read this poem, think about the following questions. You should share your answers with a partner, a small group, or your class.

- Briefly describe the area where you live.

- How well do you think you know your neighbours?

- Can you explain what any of your neighbours do for a living, or where they work?

## Meeting the text

As you read through the poem for the first time, see if you can work out the answers to these questions:

1   Who is speaking?

2   Who is she speaking about?

3   Where is the poem set?

## Local Colour

Something I'm not familiar with, the tune
of their talking, comes tumbling before them
down the stairs which (oh I forgot) it was my turn
to do again this week.
5    My neighbour and my neighbour's child. I nod, we're not on
speaking terms exactly.

I don't know much about her. Her dinners smell
different. Her husband's a busdriver,
so I believe.
10    She carries home her groceries in Grandfare bags.
though I've seen her once or twice around the corner
at Shastri's for spices and such.
(I always shop there – he's open till all hours
making good.) How does she feel?
15    Her children grow up with foreign accents,
swearing in fluent Glaswegian. Her face
is sullen. Her coat is drab plaid, hides
but for a hint at the hem, her sari's
gold embroidered gorgeousness. She has
20    a jewel in her nostril.
The golden hands with the almond nails
that push the pram turn blue
In this city's cold climate.

Liz Lochead

## Thinking through

First, share your answers to the 'Meeting the text' questions you were given at the start of the poem. Then work out the answers to the following three questions:

1   Apart from the speaker and her neighbour, which other characters feature in the poem? List them.

2   How can we tell from the poem that the speaker's neighbour is not originally from Glasgow?

3   Where do you think she has come from? (Her clothes and jewellery should give you a clue here.)

## Let's get to work

As we study this poem we are going to look mainly at how the words used by the speaker build up two pictures for us. One is of the neighbour she speaks about, but the other is the picture we get of the speaker herself.

You should have been able to work out that both of them live in the same block of tenement flats in a Scottish city. The speaker is Scottish, while her neighbour is an immigrant. The jewel in the neighbour's nostril and her sari suggest that her original home was in India, and that she is a follower of the Hindu religion.

The story 'The Test', which is also in this book, covers some similar themes in a different way. In that story, we followed the point of view of Marian, the only black person in a story full of white people. In this poem we follow the point of view of the speaker. She seems to be the only white person, while all the other characters mentioned are living in Scotland but have an Asian birth or background.

## Dramatic monologue

This type of poem is called a **dramatic monologue**. The word **monologue** tells us that someone is speaking uninterrupted, rather than taking part in a conversation. The word **dramatic** tells us that the speaker is not alone and talking to herself, but that someone else is supposedly there listening.

■   Who do you think the Scottish woman is speaking to?

One feature of dramatic monologues is that their speakers often let slip some of their nastier or more unpleasant thoughts, habits or actions. In

'Local Colour', the speaker thinks she is telling us about her Indian neighbour, but accidentally reveals a great deal about herself too. Not all of it is very nice.

We're going to look at this monologue in three parts. In each part of the monologue we'll see the writer using the same techniques: **alliteration**, **double meanings**, **word choice** and **revelation**.

# Part one: the first verse

## Alliteration

**Alliteration** is when a writer uses two or more words close together that begin with the same sound.

Alliteration is often used to focus the reader's attention on a certain area of the text, perhaps to make us notice something else that is happening there, or to get us to concentrate on a point the writer is making.

However alliteration can also affect the speed of a piece of writing. Alliteration made by repeating hard sounds such as **b**, **k**, **t** and so on can make the writing seem to speed up. For example:

> **The runners burst forward at the b of the bang**

Alliteration made by repeating soft sounds such as **f**, **m** or **s** can make the writing seem to slow down, and can produce a gentle feeling. For example:

> **The stream slowly slipped and softly slithered between the trees.**

## Now try this

Copy out the first four lines of the poem. These lines make up the first sentence. Now underline or circle the letters that create alliteration here. Remember, alliteration is a sound-effect technique, not a spelling one. Think about the sounds the letters make.

Liz Lochead does a very clever thing here. The speaker is telling us that a sound has grabbed her attention. To do this she uses alliteration, a sound-effect technique, to grab our attention and to make us notice what is happening in these two lines of the poem.

## Now try this

Answer these questions:

1 Which alliteration do we find in line 5? Quote the words.

2 What is the writer trying to focus our attention on?

3 Why does the writer want us to focus on this?

## Double meaning

Lochead uses a very particular sort of double meaning here called **ambiguity**. If something is **ambiguous** it has two possible meanings. It may be impossible for us to know which meaning is the right one, even if we can see what both those possible meanings are.

In this verse, the ambiguity is in lines 5 and 6:

> **I nod, we're not on**
>
> **speaking terms exactly.**

## Now try this

That comment has two possible meanings. It could have a neutral meaning, or a nastier one. Explain what the two possible meanings are.

## Word choice

As we study this poem we'll see that it makes careful use of **positive** and **negative word choice** at different times.

In line 1 we see an example of **positive word choice**. The speaker calls the sounds of her neighbours' speech

> **the tune of their talking**

The word 'tune' there is a positive one. It tells us something about how their speech, in a foreign language she doesn't understand, sounds to her.

■ What does it tell us about the way she feels?

The most neutral word the speaker could have used there is the word 'sound'. 'Sound' just tells us that somebody heard something, but doesn't tell us whether they liked it or not, whether they thought it was a nice sound or not.

## Now try this

Put the word 'sound' in the middle of a page. On one side, write all the words you can think of that mean nearly the same but tell us that it is a pleasant sound to hear. On the other side, write all the words you can think of that suggest a nasty or unpleasant sound. The example below will get you started. Copy it and carry on.

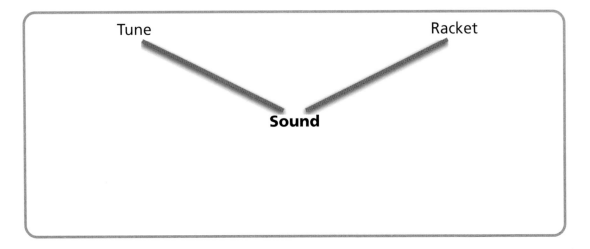

Tune        Racket

**Sound**

## Revelation

We've already discovered that, in a dramatic monologue, the speaker often ends up **revealing** things about him or herself without realising this. In this verse, the speaker **reveals** a couple of things that show her in a rather bad light.

## Now try this

Find quotations from the poem to prove:

- that the speaker is an unreliable or lazy neighbour

- that the speaker has not bothered getting to know her Indian neighbour.

After each quotation, explain in your own words how the quotation you have chosen proves the point.

By the way, the comment in brackets in line 3 is called an **aside**. This is when someone breaks off from the main subject they are talking about to mention something else which has just occurred to them. **Asides** often give away what is on someone's mind. We'll meet another of these later in the poem.

## Part two: verse two, from line 7 to the middle of line 14

### Alliteration

## Now try this

Answer these questions. Look back at the definition of alliteration given earlier if you need to.

1  Which alliteration do we find in lines 7 and 8? Quote the words. What is the writer trying to focus our attention on? Why?

2  Which alliteration do we find in line 10? Quote the words. What is the writer trying to focus our attention on? Why?

3  Which alliteration (and in fact other repetition of the same letter sound) do we find in line 12? Quote the words. What is the writer trying to focus our attention on? Why?

### Double meaning

There's another example of **ambiguity** in this section of the poem. It comes in lines 7 and 8 when the speaker says

**Her dinners smell different**

## Now try this

That comment has two possible meanings. It could have a neutral meaning, or a more nasty one. Explain what the two possible meanings are.

## Word choice and revelation

This part of the poem doesn't use the same sorts of positive and negative word choice that we see in parts one and three. Instead, in this part of the poem, word choice is used to reveal more about the speaker. It's in this part of the poem that we see her at her worst. She comes across as **someone who jumps to conclusions** and a **hypocrite**. She comes quite close to being a **racist**.

## Now try this

On the left of the table below are some quotations from the poem. On the right are their explanations. The explanations are in **the wrong order**. Copy the quotations into your notebook and beside or underneath each quotation write down what the quoted words or lines give away about the speaker.

| Quotations | What the quotations show |
|---|---|
| *Her husband's a busdriver, so I believe* | The shop belongs to someone from an ethnic minority group |
| *at Shastri's for spices and such* | She assumes he is making good money, almost taking advantage of his customers |
| *I always shop there – he's open till all hours* | The speaker has no actual proof of his job, she just assumes that Asian men tend to do certain jobs |
| *making good* | The speaker is happy to shop there because it's convenient for her |

## Now try this

Write a paragraph in your notebook to explain each of the following things. Use quotations and other evidence from the poem in each paragraph.

1 that the speaker jumps to conclusions, or makes assumptions without good evidence

2 that the speaker is a hypocrite

3 that the speaker comes close to being a racist

4 how the author uses another example of **an aside** to show what the speaker is like (We already saw one use of an aside in the first section of the poem.)

## Part three: the middle of line 14 to the end of the poem

### Alliteration

## Now try this

Answer these questions. Look back at the definition of alliteration given earlier if you need to.

1 Which alliteration do we find in lines 17 and 18? Quote the words. What is the writer trying to focus our attention on? Why?

2 Which alliteration do we find in lines 19 to 21? Quote the words. What is the writer trying to focus our attention on? Why?

3 Which alliteration do we find in the last line? Quote the words. What is the writer trying to focus our attention on? Why?

### Double meaning

This time the double meaning isn't an example of **ambiguity**, which is when both meanings are possible but we can't tell which meaning the speaker intends. This time the double meanings are both true at the same time, but in different ways.

The double meaning comes at the very end of the poem when the speaker tells us about:

**this city's cold climate**

One of the meanings is a **literal meaning**. It is actually, factually true.

The other one is a **metaphorical meaning**. It is true in a wider, deeper, more thoughtful sort of way.

## Now try this

Copy the following paragraph and fill in the gaps to explain the double meaning in the final line of the poem.

*At the very end of the poem the speaker tells us that her Indian neighbour pushes her pram through, '_____.' These words have a literal meaning. They tell us that _____. The words also have a metaphorical meaning. They suggest that _____.*

## Word choice

In this part of the poem the speaker again uses some words with **positive connotations** and others with **negative connotations**. (Connotations are the ideas and suggestions that something sets off in our mind.)

What's interesting is that all these words, both the positive ones and the negative ones, are about what the Indian woman looks like.

Let's look first at the negative word choice. We're going to focus on two words in line 17, 'sullen' and 'drab'. These negative words tell us about how the new environment of Glasgow affects her and affects the way she looks.

## Now try this

Use a dictionary. Look up the two words quoted above. Write each word in your notebook and, beside the word, write its meaning. Underneath the meaning, write a sentence of your own to prove to yourself that you understand what the word means.

Then answer the following question:

■ What do these two words, *sullen* and *drab*, tell us about how living in Glasgow affects this Indian neighbour?

Now we're going to look at the positive word choice in this section. The positive words describe the way the Indian neighbour chooses to look, the way she decides to present herself. Many of these details are connected to the fact that she still dresses in the way she would in her home country, rather than just blending in with the Glaswegians around her.

## Now try this

Answer these three questions:

1  Which four words in the last five lines of the poem have particularly positive connotations?

2  Three of these words all belong to the same area of language. Which of the three words go together? What is the connection between them?

3  What, in particular, do these three words tell us about the way the speaker feels about her neighbour's looks?

## Now try this

As best as you can (don't worry, this is English, not art) draw a picture of the woman the poem describes. Use the description in lines 14 to 22 to help you. Label the drawing with quotations from the poem. Use black or dark ink for the negative quotations, and red or brightly coloured ink for the positive quotations.

## Revelation

So far the speaker in the poem has not given us a very flattering picture of herself. However, in this final section, we see her in a better light, as she actually begins to take a genuine interest in her neighbour.

### Now try this

Copy the following three paragraphs in to your notebook. Use quotations from the poem and explanations in your own words to help you keep a note of what is revealed about the speaker in this final section of the poem.

*In the last section of the poem, the speaker shows some sympathy for her Indian neighbour. In line 14 she asks herself a question about her neighbour: '_____?' This shows her trying to understand her neighbour's point of view. The speaker's sympathy seems to be aroused by the fact that _____.*

*In the last section of the poem the speaker also seems to be taking an interest in her neighbour. This is shown by the way she describes the woman's looks. She notices attractive details, such as '_____' and '_____', and also negative details, such as '_____ and '_____'.*

*The speaker seems at last to find her neighbour special and valuable. I know this because [**use a mixture of quotation from the poem and explanation in your own words to complete this part of your explanation**]. So, in the end, we see a better side of the speaker.*

## The turning point

That concludes our trip through the three sections of the poem. However, you may be wondering why we divided the poem into these sections. The poem is only split into two, not three, verses after all.

The reason we split the second verse of 'Local Colour' into two parts is because it contains the **turning point** of the poem.

A **turning point** is the point after which everything is different. We often find turning points in literature. In Shakespeare's play *Romeo and*

*Juliet* everything is going well for the two young lovers until about half way through the play. In just one short scene, two people are killed and Romeo is banished far away. After that, everything goes wrong for the young lovers.

We can find turning points in life too. Someone might have a hard life with a tough upbringing, but the turning point might come when he leaves home and starts mixing with new people. For some people, going to university is a turning point in life. After they've been there, they get opportunities in life they'd never have had otherwise.

In 'Local Colour', the turning point comes in line 12 when the speaker asks:

**How does she feel?**

**?**

Two important things change after the turning point. First, the mood or tone of the poem changes. Secondly, we start to get a very different, and nicer, picture of the speaker.

## Now try this

Copy the following table into your notebook and complete it to show how these things are different before and after the turning point.

*'How does she feel?'*

|  | What the speaker seems to be like | Mood or tone of the poem |
|---|---|---|
| Before turning point |  |  |
| After turning point |  |  |

## Themes

A major theme in this poem is **isolation**. The Indian woman is isolated, cut off, in lots of different ways and for lots of different reasons.

## Now try this

You may want to work as a group on this task. If you do, you should present your answers to the class as a poster, a PowerPoint, or an overhead. Start with the basic spider plan below. For each spider leg, add details, explanations and quotations to show either **how** the woman is isolated or **why** she is isolated. You may also wish to add other legs to the spider.

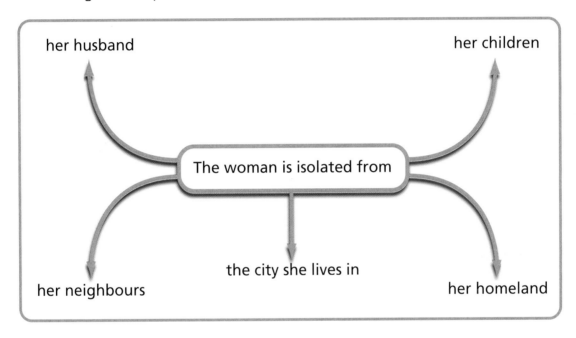

## First person

This poem is written in the first person. In other words, it is written using words the *I* voice. The person telling us the poem is also somehow involved in it.

In some ways this is very useful. It feels as if the speaker is talking directly to us, which brings the poem to life. However, it makes the poem very **subjective**. In other words, we only see things from one point of view. We can only know as much as the speaker knows. She doesn't know much for sure. She admits this in line 6:

> **I don't know much about her**

which doesn't stop her telling us about her neighbour for the whole of the rest of the poem.

## Now try this

You are going to explore the other point of view, that of the Indian woman. You will write what you think she wants to say about her white neighbour, about her family, and about her new life in Glasgow. Try to express how you think she feels. Start with:

*I passed that woman from downstairs today. . .*

## Possible essay tasks

Now that you've finished studying this poem, you could tackle the following essay questions. Remember to follow the advice from the chapter on how to write literature essays.

Above the poetry essay choices on the exam paper you will see the following words:

> **Answers to questions in this section should refer to the text and such relevant features as: word choice, tone, imagery, structure, content, rhythm, theme, sound, ideas . . .**

Now look at the essay choices:

- Choose a poem which starts with a description of a small event or everyday incident but which then explores more serious issues.

  Discuss how effectively the poet uses the initial particular incident to lead to a general or universal statement.

or

- Choose a poem which successfully describes a person, or a place, or an animal.

  Show how the important features of the subject of the poem are illustrated in such a way as to make an impact on you.

or

- Choose a poem in which a character or an incident or an experience is vividly described.

  Briefly state what the poem is about and go on to say what techniques are used in the poem to catch and maintain your interest.

or

- Choose a poem which makes you feel pity or sympathy for a person or an animal.

  Show how both the content and the style of the poem create pity or sympathy.

# 7

# Poetry: My Parents Kept Me from Children Who Were Rough

 **Getting in**

You're about to read a poem. The writer tells us about his experience of being bullied as a child. Before you read the poem, think about the following questions. You might feel able to share your answers with a partner, a small group, or your class. However, some of these questions are quite personal. It's fine if you want to keep your answers to yourself.

- Have you, at any point in your life, been bullied? What happened? How did it make you feel?

- Have you, at any point in your life, been a bully? Why do you think you did this?

- Have you, at any point in your life, been aware that a friend was being bullied? What happened? How did it make you feel? Did you get involved?

- Why do you think certain people become bullies?

- Why do you think certain people end up as victims?

 **Meeting the text**

As you read through the story for the first time, make a list of all the different things the group of bullies did to Spender when he was young. You should divide your list into three sections:

1 Physical bullying: things they did that hurt his body

2 Psychological bullying: things they did that hurt his feelings

3 Social bullying: things they did that made him feel left out

## My Parents Kept Me from Children Who Were Rough

My parents kept me from children who were rough
And who threw words like stones and who wore torn clothes.
Their thighs showed through rags. They ran in the street
4    And climbed cliffs and stripped by the country streams.

I feared more than tigers their muscles like iron
And their jerking hands and their knees tight on my arms.
I feared the salt coarse pointing of those boys
8    Who copied my lisp behind me on the road.

They were lithe, they sprang out behind hedges
Like dogs to bark at our world. They threw mud
And I looked the other way, pretending to smile.
12    I longed to forgive them, yet they never smiled.

Stephen Spender

##  Thinking through

First, share your answers to the 'Meeting the Text' questions you were given at the start of the poem. Then work out the answers to the following four questions. They are all quite **speculative**. In other words, they ask you what you think, but different people may have different opinions about the answers. Make sure you can back up your opinions with evidence from the poem.

1 Why do you think the other children bullied Spender?

2 How old do you think the children all were when this happened?

3 Do you think the bullies were ever punished?

4 Do you think Spender's parents knew about the bullying?

##  Let's get to work

As we study this poem we are going to look mainly at two things:

■ the way Spender describes the bullies and their actions

■ the emotions he felt while he was being bullied.

In both cases we'll see how Spender uses certain techniques to put these across.

To keep things clear, when we are thinking about young Stephen Spender, the little boy who was bullied by a gang of other boys; we'll refer to him as **Stephen**. If we want to discuss the adult poet, or the techniques in his writing, we'll talk about **Spender**.

## The bullies and their actions

### Social class

The word *'rough'* in line 1 is an important one in this poem. First of all, it does describe the bullies and their behaviour. However, it also tells us something about Stephen Spender's family. It's probably not a word the young Stephen thought of by himself. It's much more likely that he thought the other boys were 'rough' because he had heard his parents describing them that way. His parents have judged those boys, and then passed their ideas about them on to Stephen.

In fact there seems to be a big difference in social class between Stephen's family and the families of the other boys.

British society is very class based. When we talk about class we are talking about a whole lot of complex factors. The more you know about someone, the more accurately you can pinpoint their class.

### Now try this

Copy and complete the following table. Fill in what you think would describe a person in each class. Some suggestions are already in place to help you.

| Details | Working class | Middle class |
|---|---|---|
| **Job** | | doctor, lawyer |
| **Goes on holiday to** | Magaluf, Tenerife | |
| **Level of education** | | |
| **Car driven** | | BMW, Mercedes |
| **Favourite drink** | | |
| **Buys clothes in** | Matalan | |
| **Hobbies** | | |
| **Names for children** | | |
| **Lives in** | | |
| **Reads this newspaper** | | |

Of course class is not really that simple. Lots of people with university degrees still end up in poorly paid jobs. Lots of working class people buy expensive clothes. It's important not to leap to quick conclusions. Nobody likes to feel judged.

Let's go back to those 'rough' boys.

## Now try this

Answer the following questions:

1 Look at verse 1. Quote two expressions which show the boys' families were quite poor.

2 Look at verse 1. Find two harmless things the other boys did which Stephen's parents probably disapproved of or did not want him to do.

3 Look at verse 3. Quote the expression that tells us Stephen felt there was a big social difference between his family and the other boys.

As we said above, nobody likes to feel judged. That may be why Stephen's problems started. Perhaps the other boys heard Stephen, or his parents, describing them as 'rough' and didn't like it. Perhaps they were very aware of the differences between themselves and the Spenders. Most bullying is based on somebody picking on somebody else because the victim somehow seems different from the bully.

## Similes

A **simile** is a description made by using the word **like** or the word **as**. For example:

> **She's got a voice like a foghorn**

or

> **He's about as useful as a chocolate teapot**

Spender uses one simile in each verse of the poem. The similes allow him to give us a vivid picture of the bullies and their actions.

## Now try this

Copy and complete the table.

| Verse | The simile | What the simile tells us |
|-------|-----------|--------------------------|
| 1 | | |
| 2 | | |
| 3 | | |

## Allusion

One of these similes, the one in verse 1, is also an example of a technique called **allusion**. **Allusion** is when a writer makes a brief reference to something, or hints at something, that he thinks we will recognise or remember.

## Now try this

Copy and complete this paragraph in your notebook. You may want to discuss the answer with your group or class before you write.

*In verse 1 Spender uses a simile and tells us that the boys '_____'. This simile is also an example of the technique of _____ . Spender is alluding to the well-known saying '_____'.*

*I think Spender agrees/disagrees [Choose the right word] with this saying. I think this because . . . [Carry on the explanation in your own words.]*

There's another example of allusion in verse 2 when Spender says:

**I feared the salt coarse pointing of those boys**

This time he's alluding to the expression

**rubbing salt into the wound**

## Now try this

Answer these questions.

1　If you had a wound such as a cut, how would it feel if you got salt into it?

2　What, therefore, does the expression 'rubbing salt into the wound' mean or suggest?

3　Why does Spender describe the boys' pointing as 'salt'?

## Other descriptions of the bullies

You should know that a **verb** is a doing word. Verbs tell us what someone or something does, or did. Spender chooses the verbs in the poem very carefully.

## Now try this

Read through the poem. As you do so, collect all the verbs that tell us anything the bullies did. You can ignore any verbs that tell us about Stephen or his parents. Copy and complete the table below, putting the verbs into three separate columns, one for each verse.

| Verse 1 | Verse 2 | Verse 3 |
|---------|---------|---------|
| Threw   |         |         |

Now look again at the verbs you have collected. Draw a circle round each one that makes the boys sound very active, or lively, or physically fit.

You should have noticed that a high proportion of the verbs used about the boys make them sound very fit, active or lively. The boys come across as rather vibrant, if also rather scary, characters.

Spender also describes the boys in ways which make them sound like animals. In line 10 he describes them as:

**like dogs**

In line 9 he says that

**They were lithe**

The word 'lithe' means fit, agile, moving easily. It's a word we might often use to describe some freely moving animal like a cat, or maybe even a snake.

You might also agree that the phrase

**they sprang out**

also makes them sound more like animals than humans.

Now that you've thought about these active verbs, and these words and phrases with animal connotations, you should be able to answer this question:

■ WHY does Spender chose to describe the boys in this way?

## Spender's feelings

### Fear

Look back at the list you made at the start of this chapter of all the things the bullies did to Stephen.

■ Which verse of the poem are most of these things mentioned in?

Because this verse contains most of the bullying, this verse also tells us most about the very understandable fear Stephen felt. He uses the phrase, 'I feared . . .' twice in this verse.

### Now try this

List the four things Spender says he was afraid of.

### Unexpected emotions

It's not surprising that Stephen was afraid of the bullies. However some of the other feelings in the poem are a bit more unexpected. During the poem he expresses, as well as fear, **envy**, **loneliness** and even **forgiveness**.

#### Envy

In verse 1, Spender tells us that the rough children:

> ran in the street
>
> And climbed cliffs, and stripped by the country streams

Nowadays lots of parents might not want their children to behave like this. In the 1920s, when Spender was growing up, parents were not quite so anxious about what children, especially boys, got up to. It would have been entirely normal for little boys to be climbing cliffs, or swimming naked.

Spender goes further than just mentioning what the boys did, he draws our attention to it by using **alliteration**. (If you don't remember what this is, look back at the explanation in the chapter about the poem 'Local Colour'.) The alliterations here are quite clever and complex, based on sounds that are made by groups of letters, not just single letters.

**climbed cliffs    stripped . . . streams**

All this attention on the boys' behaviour seems to be because Stephen envies them. Spender points out all the things they were allowed to do because he wanted to do those things too when he was a boy. If his parents thought those boys were 'rough', then they would certainly never have let Stephen do the things those boys did.

### Loneliness and forgiveness

These two feelings come up in the last verse.

### Now try this

1   Copy and complete the table below to prove and explain how we find these two emotions in the last verse.

| Loneliness | Forgiveness |
|---|---|
| Quotation: | Quotation: |
| Explanation: | Explanation: |

2   Why do you think Stephen felt lonely? Make your answer as full as possible.

3   Why do you think Stephen wanted to forgive the boys? Make your answer as full as possible.

These two emotions in the last verse help to change or widen out the mood of the poem. When we read about what the bullies did to Spender we feel sorry for him, and probably also angry with the bullies. The emotions in the last verse, and especially in the final two lines of the poem, make it a very sad one as well.

## Bringing it all together

To help you demonstrate your knowledge and understanding of the poem, work on these two tasks.

### Now try this

Decide on one or two themes you believe Spender is exploring in the poem. For each theme you identify, write a paragraph to explain why you believe that to be a theme of the poem. Justify your ideas with quotations from the text and references to it.

## Now try this

You're going to explore the other point of view, that of the group of rough boys. Write what you think they would say about Stephen and his family. Start with:

*That boy Stephen Spender lives up the street from us. . .*

## Possible essay tasks

Now that you've finished studying this poem, you could tackle the following essay questions. Remember to follow the advice from the chapter on how to write literature essays.

Above the poetry essay choices on the exam paper you will see the following words:

> **Answers to questions in this section should refer to the text and such relevant features as: word choice, tone, imagery, structure, content, rhythm, theme, sound, ideas . . .**

Now look at the essay choices:

- Choose a poem in which a particular mood such as joy, anger or sorrow is created.

  State what the mood is and show how the poet has created it effectively for you.

or

- Choose a poem which deals with an aspect of the less pleasant side of life.

  Show how the poem increases your knowledge and understanding of the aspect of life dealt with and how the use of poetic technique contributes to the impact the poem had on you.

or

■ Choose a poem in which a character or an incident or an experience is vividly described.

Briefly state what the poem is about and go on to say what techniques are used in the poem to catch and maintain your interest.

or

■ Choose a poem which makes you feel pity or sympathy for a person or an animal.

Show how both the content and the style of the poem create pity or sympathy.

# 8 | Poetry: Telephone Conversation

 **Getting in**

This poem describes what happened to the speaker when he tried to rent a room. Before you read the poem, think about the following questions. You should share your answers with a partner, a small group, or your class.

- Have you ever had a really awkward or uncomfortable telephone conversation? What was the conversation about?

- Have you ever felt that someone judged you as soon as they met you, without getting to know you properly?

 **Meeting the text**

As you read through the poem for the first time, do this:

- Make a note of very time you find a word which describes a colour, or a particular shade of a colour.

## Telephone Conversation

The price seemed reasonable, location
Indifferent. The landlady swore she lived
Off premises. Nothing remained
4    But self-confession. 'Madam,' I warned,
'I hate a wasted journey – I am African.'
Silence. Silenced transmission of
Pressurised good breeding. Voice, when it came,
8    Lipstick-coated, long gold-rolled
Cigarette-holder pipped. Caught I was, foully.
'HOW DARK?' . . . I had not misheard . . . 'ARE YOU LIGHT
OR VERY DARK?' Button B. Button A. Stench
12    Of rancid breath of public hide and speak.
Red booth. Red pillar box. Red double-tiered
Omnibus squelching tar. It *was* real! Shamed
By ill-mannered silence, surrender
16    Pushed dumbfoundment to beg simplification.
Considerate she was, varying the emphasis -
'ARE YOU DARK? OR VERY LIGHT?' Revelation came.
'You mean – like plain or milk chocolate?'
20    Her assent was clinical, crushing in its light
Impersonality. Rapidly, wave-length adjusted.
I chose. 'West African sepia' – and as an afterthought,
'Down in my passport.' Silence for spectroscopic
24    Flight of fancy, till truthfulness clanged her accent
Hard on the mouthpiece. 'WHAT'S THAT?' conceding
'DON'T KNOW WHAT THAT IS.' 'Like brunette.'
'THAT'S DARK, ISN'T IT?' 'Not altogether.
28    Facially I am brunette, but madam, you should see
The rest of me. Palm of my hand, soles of my feet
Are a peroxide blond. Friction caused –
Foolishly, madam – by sitting down, has turned
My bottom raven black – One moment, madam!' – sensing
33    Her receiver rearing on the thunderclap
About my ear – 'Madam,' I pleaded, 'wouldn't you rather
See for yourself?'

Wole Soyinka

 **Thinking through**

First, share your answers to the 'Meeting the Text' questions you were given at the start of the poem. Then work out the answers to the following three tasks. You may wish to work with a partner or a small group.

1   In a few sentences, describe what happens in the poem.

2   In a few sentences, describe what you know about the narrator.

3   In a few sentences, describe what you know about the landlady.

 **Let's get to work**

As we study this poem we are going to look mainly at how Soyinka uses various techniques, especially **word choice**, to create a clear picture of the two characters, and of the incident they are involved in.

Before we do this, it will be helpful if you know a bit about Soyinka himself, and about the time at which the poem is set.

Wole Soyinka was born in Nigeria, Africa, in 1934. He studied at Nigeria's most elite high school and in 1954 came to Britain to attend university in Leeds, where he received an honours degree in English Literature. While at Leeds he was well known for his sharp tongue and his wit. He has since spent most of his life as a university teacher and writer, and won the Nobel Prize for Literature in 1984.

All these facts show that Soyinka is a highly intelligent man, and a skilled user of the English language. However, when he lived in Britain in the 1950s, many people would have been surprised to find out that a black person could be like this. Britain was not very ethnically mixed, and many people had never met a non-white person. Even in areas where there were black people, this did not mean they were welcome. Lots of houses with rooms to rent would have had signs at the door saying 'No blacks'. This attitude shocks us now, but it's the kind of attitude the landlady in this poem has.

This poem seems to be based on a real experience Soyinka had when trying to rent a room. What's more, it doesn't seem to be about his only bad experience.

## Now try this

Read the first five lines of the poem again.

1  How can you tell the speaker has had bad experiences with landladies before?

2  What exactly do you think had happened to him before?

3  How does he try to make things work out differently this time?

## Lines 1–9

This first part of the poem sets up the situation and includes Soyinka's 'confession' of his race.

### Word choice

In this part of the poem certain words have been chosen because of their **connotations** – the ideas and feelings they suggest to us. For example when Soyinka tells us that:

> The price seemed **reasonable**, location
> **Indifferent**

the two words printed in bold make the room Soyinka wants to rent sound good, but not wonderful. They are very **neutral, non-committal words**. This has deeper connotations. Soyinka is probably trying not to get too excited or enthusiastic about the room, in case he does end up being rejected because of his skin colour. If he decided the room sounded wonderful, then the disappointment of being turned down would be worse.

## Now try this

Look at the following words and phrases quoted from this first section of the poem. For each quotation, decide what the connotations are. Use the hints to help you.

| Quotation | Hint |
|---|---|
| *Off premises* | What does this say about the landlady's involvement? |
| *self-confession* | Think about the negative connotations of this word. |
| *African* | What does this tell us (and the landlady) about Soyinka? Why does he not use a more obvious, direct word? |
| *pressurised* | How genuine is the landlady's *good breeding* at this point in the poem? |

The wording Soyinka uses to describe the landlady's voice is also interesting. Remember that he never actually sees or meets this woman. All that he ever knows about her comes through the medium of her voice. Throughout the poem he uses the sounds of her voice, and the words she says, to help him to imagine what she looks like. Everything he says about her appearance is made up, or is a guess based on evidence he hears in her speech.

He describes her voice as:

> **Lipstick coated, long gold-rolled**
> **Cigarette-holder pipped.**

When Soyinka pictures the landlady, he imagines her as the kind of woman who'd use a cigarette holder like the one in the picture on the right. By carrying the cigarette in a holder a smoker could keep tell-tale yellow nicotine stains off her fingers. In a way, anyone using a cigarette holder was hiding something about herself.

In Soyinka's imagined picture of the landlady, even the cigarette holder itself is a bit fake. The words 'gold-rolled' tells us that, although it looks as if it's made of gold, it's actually made of a cheap metal with a very thin layer of gold on top. This goes with his description of the woman's voice as 'coated' in lipstick. Not that there's anything wrong with wearing lipstick, but Soyinka is already picturing the woman as someone who seems to be something she is not. And remember, he gets all of this just from the sound of her voice.

## Repetition

When Soyinka confesses to being African he hears

> **'Silence. Silenced transmission of**
> **Pressurised good breeding.'**

This near repetition of the word 'silence' tells us that the landlady was quiet for a very long time – rather awkward during a phone call.

■  What does this reveal about her feelings at this point?

## Sentence structure

This part of the poem ends with the sentence

> **Caught I was, foully.**

Soyinka has changed the normal order that you would expect the words of this sentence to go in.

## Now try this

1  What order should the words of this sentence go in? Rewrite the sentence as it would normally be written.

2  What effect does Soyinka gain by changing the order of the words in the sentence?

## Lines 10–18

This section of the poem begins with the landlady's shocking question and goes on to show Soyinka's amazement at what he has been asked.

### Capital letters

Whenever the landlady speaks in the poem, Soyinka shows this in capital letters. There are three reasons for this.

## Now try this

Copy and complete the table below to explain Soyinka's use of capitals.

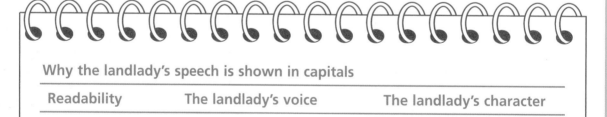

| Why the landlady's speech is shown in capitals | | |
| --- | --- | --- |
| Readability | The landlady's voice | The landlady's character |
| | | |

## Real-life details

Soyinka is amazed by the landlady's question about the precise shade of his skin. It is an astonishing question. It's as if there might be a shade of blackness that would make his skin colour acceptable and get him the room, but if he were one shade darker that would be too much and she would not give him the room.

To get over his shock, Soyinka looks around him to remind himself that all of this is real. Not only is it real, it isn't very nice. First he examines the phone box:

> **Button B. Button A. Stench**
> **Of rancid breath of public hide and speak.**

(The options Button B or Button A were given in old-fashioned phone boxes, to either connect or cancel a call when somebody answered.)

At the start of the poem, through words like *reasonable* and *indifferent*, Soyinka used **neutral, non-committal word choice**. At that stage he was feeling quietly optimistic about getting the room. Now that his chances are getting worse, the word choice is more **negative**.

■ Which words in the above quotation are particularly negative?

■ Why do you think he calls the phone box a 'hide and speak'?

Next, Soyinka looks outside the phone box.

He sees:

> **Red booth. Red pillar box. Red double-tiered**
> **Omnibus squelching tar.**

At first this just seems to be a description of what he saw outside the phone box. However it also uses **repetition** to create a very clever

**allusion**, and contains a very clever **image** in which objects are used as **symbols**.

Let's look first at the **allusion**. This technique means making a subtle reference that brings something to mind. Soyinka continually sees red:

> **Red booth. Red pillar box. Red double-tiered Omnibus**

- What do we mean if we say that we 'see red'?

- What does the continual reference to seeing red objects tell us about how Soyinka is feeling?

Now let's look at the image, and the symbols it contains. Soyinka sees a:

> **Red double-tiered**
> **Omnibus squelching tar.**

Imagine a Hollywood movie set in London. The film makers very often use a shot of a red double-decker bus to establish the setting. (The Austin Powers films send this up brilliantly.) The red bus has become a stereotypical symbol for London. Soyinka takes this further, and uses the bus as a symbol not just for London, but for Britain, and a particular British person.

## Now try this

Copy and complete the following paragraph into your notebook.

*In the image of the* **[quote the image]** *the various details are symbols. The bus stands for* _____ *because* **[complete the explanation]**. *The tar stands for* _____ *because* **[complete the explanation]**. *The fact that the tar is being squelched tells us what the landlady is doing to Soyinka. She is* **[complete the explanation]**. *The fact that the tar is being squelched also tells us how Soyinka feels. He is feeling* **[complete the explanation]**.

## Word choice

The writer's word choice here tells us more about his personality and upbringing. Eventually, after staring around for some time, Soyinka begins to feel 'shamed' by what he describes as his own 'ill-mannered silence'.

- Why is it **ironic** that he describes himself as 'ill-mannered'?

- What does the fact that he feels this way tell us about his personality and upbringing?

In this part of the poem Soyinka also uses **emotive language**, words that are strong and powerful and arouse our emotions as we read them. He tells us that at this stage he had to 'surrender' and that he had to 'beg' her to simplify the question. Her question isn't actually very complicated. It's more that the question is so amazing that Soyinka can't believe she really means it. Meanwhile the emotive words 'surrender' and 'beg' tell us that he feels completely powerless at this stage in the telephone conversation.

Finally, the writer uses **sarcasm**.

## Now try this

Read the quotation below, and then answer the questions that follow.

> Considerate she was, varying the emphasis
>
> 'ARE YOU DARK? OR VERY LIGHT?'

1 Which word used by Soyinka is particularly sarcastic?

2 Why is this word sarcastic, and not genuine?

3 How would **you** describe the landlady's actions at this point in the poem?

4 If you had to choose just one word to describe the landlady at this point, what would it be?

# Lines 18–27

## Word choice

In this part of the poem Soyinka begins to fight back, using his better vocabulary. An important word in showing the turnaround at this point is 'Revelation' at the end of line 18.

■ What does this word mean?

Now that Soyinka at last understands the situation, he takes control of it.

He asks the landlady

**You mean like plain or milk chocolate?**

In using this **simile**, Soyinka is being sarcastic again. When we saw him using sarcasm in line 17 he was doing this after the event – talking to us, the readers, in a sarcastic way. This time he's using sarcasm during the actual telephone call itself. The landlady's question is a stupid one, but the topic of the colour of someone's skin, and how they are treated because of it, is a serious one. By comparing it to something as trivial as the colours of two sorts of chocolate, Soyinka is being highly sarcastic, while still giving the woman the impression that he is playing along with her question.

When she agrees that that is the kind of thing she means, Soyinka tells her he is 'West African sepia' adding that these words are 'Down in my passport'.

It's at this stage that we start to see how clever the writer is, and how ignorant the woman is. First of all, she doesn't know what 'sepia' means.

■ What does *sepia* mean?

■ Why do you think Soyinka wanted her to know these words were in his passport? How might saying this strengthen his case?

■ What is the landlady doing when the writer says she is a having a 'spectroscopic flight of fancy'?

Earlier on, we noticed how, just from the sound of her voice at the start of the call, Soyinka pictured this woman as rather fake, someone pretending be something she is not. Now we start to realise that he was right about this. He tells us in line 24 that:

**truthfulness clanged her accent
Hard on the mouthpiece**

- *What* happened to the landlady's voice at this stage in the conversation?

- *Why* did this happen to her voice at this point?

Now the landlady is forced to admit her ignorance. She asks,

**WHAT'S THAT? . . . DON'T KNOW WHAT THAT IS**

When Soyinka answers, he chooses his comparison carefully, telling her he is 'brunette'.

- What does the word 'brunette' mean?

- There is only one thing we would ever describe as being brunette. What is it?

By using the word 'brunette' as a description of his skin, Soyinka is suggesting that the landlady is very shallow, only interested in how people look on the outside, and that she is a very stupid person who only understands unimportant things like hair dye.

## Lines 28 to the end

In this final section Soyinka's wit means that, although he doesn't get the room, he does win a moral victory over the landlady. He probably knows by now that she will never rent the room to him, so he can be as subversive as he likes.

First he points out how stupid her question about the shade of his skin is, demonstrating that if they followed her logic, some parts of his body would be allowed to stay in her house while other parts would not.

> Facially I am brunette, but madam, you should see
> The rest of me. Palm of my hand, soles of my feet
> Are a peroxide blond.

Secondly, he makes one more dig about her being a fake.

- What is peroxide usually used for?

- If we describe a person as a 'peroxide blond', what do we mean?

- By introducing the word 'peroxide' into the poem, what does Soyinka tell us about the mental picture he has of the landlady?

Thirdly, although his words on the surface still seem very polite, Soyinka actually manages to insult her by making a very rude suggestion.

- Which word is used four times in the last eight lines of the poem?

- What impression of Soyinka is given by the fact that he continually repeats this word?

The last two lines of the poem contain a very **ambiguous** question. When Soyinka asks

'wouldn't you rather
See for yourself?'

this could have two meanings, one pleading and polite, one very rude.

## Now try this

Starting by quoting that question Soyinka asks, write a paragraph in your notebook to explain clearly what the two different possible meanings of this ambiguous question are.

## Now try this

Thinking back over the poem as a whole, make two lists. In one, list all the ways Soyinka has beaten the landlady, or won. In the other, list all the ways in which we might say Soyinka has lost.

## Now try this

Complete the following spine and rib diagram to show as many contrasts as possible between Soyinka and the landlady. Some categories are there for you – see how many more of your own you can add to the spine.

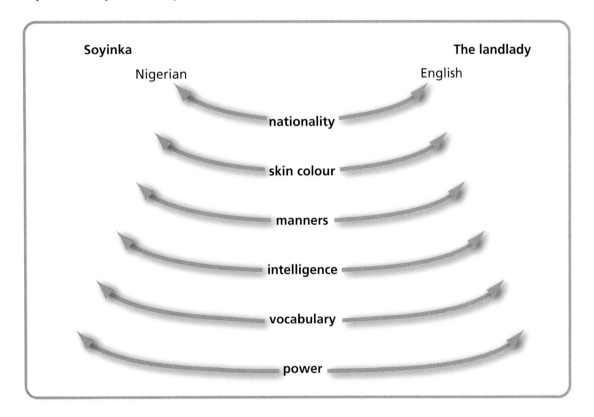

Soyinka — Nigerian

The landlady — English

nationality

skin colour

manners

intelligence

vocabulary

power

## Possible essay tasks

Now that you've finished studying this poem, you could tackle the following essay questions. Remember to follow the advice from the chapter on how to write literature essays.

Above the poetry essay choices on the exam paper you will see the following words:

> Answers to questions in this section should refer to the text and such relevant features as: word choice, tone, imagery, structure, content, rhythm, theme, sound, ideas . . .

Now look at the essay choices:

- Choose a poem in which a particular mood such as joy, anger or sorrow is created.

  State what the mood is and show how the poet has created it effectively for you.

or

- Choose a poem which deals with an aspect of the less pleasant side of life.

  Show how the poem increases your knowledge and understanding of the aspect of life dealt with, and how the use of poetic technique contributes to the impact the poem had on you.

or

- Choose a poem in which a character or an incident or an experience is vividly described.

  Briefly state what the poem is about and go on to say what techniques are used in the poem to catch and maintain your interest.

# 9 The Critical Essay

The final assessment for the Intermediate 2 course is made up of two exams which you will sit in May.

The first of these is the **Close Reading** exam, which is dealt with in another chapter of this book. The second exam paper is called the **Critical Essay**.

If you did Standard Grade then you've been examined already on your skill in writing Critical Essays. The Folio that you sent away to the examiners contained two or three of these. In Critical Essays you have to show your knowledge and understanding of a text that you have studied. You should also be able to explain some of the ways in which the author achieved what he or she wanted to with that text.

There are several important differences between the way you tackled these essays at Standard Grade and the way you will need to approach them now at Intermediate. Instead of having lots of support from your teacher to write and redraft your essays, you now have to learn to do them alone. You need to know everything there is to know about your literature texts, and choose the right details from that knowledge to use in the exam. Instead of having lots of time to work on your essays, you'll be marked on work that you do once, under exam conditions, and very quickly. The bad news (don't worry, everything gets less scary after the first time you hear this) is that in the exam you have to write two essays in 90 minutes. That's just 45 minutes each!

Why do the examiners want you to write an essay? What do they want you to prove about your skills?

They are actually looking at four different areas of your essay-writing skill: **understanding, analysis, evaluation** and **expression**.

- **Understanding** means how well you understand and know the text you have studied
- **Analysis** means being able to examine the way the writer writes and the techniques he or she uses
- **Evaluation** means having a personal response to and a personal opinion about what you have read.

■ **Expression** is how well you use the English language in your writing. This includes your spelling, grammar and punctuation. It also means that your essay has to be well linked together, and that the language you use should be formal.

As you work through this chapter you will learn to produce essays that display all these skills.

Let's start by looking at how the Critical Essay exam paper is organised. It comes in the form of a four-page booklet.

■ The front page has the name and date of the exam, and tells you the start and finish times. It will also remind you to, 'Answer **two** questions', and tells you that each is worth up to 25 marks.

■ The middle pages contain the essay choices most pupils are most likely to choose from.

■ The back page contains essay choices in two categories that not so many pupils study.

## Choosing an essay

The wording of the exam paper changed from the year 2006 onwards, and is a little different from some of the past papers you may see. At the top of the second page you'll find a general instruction like this:

**The following will be assessed:**

■ **the relevance of your essay to the question you have chosen**

■ **your knowledge and understanding of key elements, central concerns and significant details of chosen texts**

■ **your explanation of ways in which aspects of structure/style/language contribute to the meaning/effect/impact of the chosen texts**

■ **your evaluation of the effectiveness of the chosen texts, supported by detailed and relevant evidence**

■ **the quality and technical accuracy of your writing**

This is all just another way of telling you about the skills that the examiners are assessing.

The essay choices are divided into five sections from A to E like this:

Section A – Drama
Section B – Prose
Section C – Poetry

Section D – Film And TV Drama
Section E – Language

At the start of each section you will see specific advice for that type of essay. We will find out more about that later in this chapter. **The two essays you choose must come from different sections of the exam paper.**

Not many schools prepare their pupils to write about Film and TV Drama and even fewer encourage their pupils to study for the Language option. Most pupils sitting Intermediate study a mixture of poetry, plays, short stories and novels. You can write about plays in the Drama section. The short stories and novels you learn about in class are Prose. Since all the texts in this book are poems or short stories all the examples from now on will come from the Poetry and Prose sections of the exam papers. This is just so that we can base our examples on work you will find in other parts of this book. The techniques you will learn should, however, help you to write about any kind of written text that you have studied this year.

Under each of the five headings you will see three essay choices. This means that if you have studied one play, one piece of prose and one poem then there will be nine possible essays for you to pick from. But remember, you only have to write two. How are you going to make your choice?

To begin to work this out, we need to look at the way the individual questions are worded.

All the essays tasks follow the same pattern. They are set out in two paragraphs. Here's an essay task from a recent exam:

> **Choose a novel or a short story in which there is an obvious climax or turning point.**
>
> **Show how the writer leads up to this turning point or climax, and say what is its significance for the rest of the story.**

To choose which essay to write you're going to look at just the **first paragraph** of the essay topic.

As soon as you see these words, you need to run through a quick mental checklist. Let's assume you go into the exam knowing all the stories and poems in this book. You can ask yourself:

**Have I studied a novel?**

to which the answer would be:

**No.**

That doesn't mean you have to rule out trying this essay. The next thing you need to ask yourself is:

**Have I studied any short stories?**

This time the answer is:

**Yes, three of them: 'The Test', 'Death of a Spinster' and 'If I Quench Thee'.**

So you **might** be able to write this essay. Now it's time to focus in even tighter on that first paragraph and look at **what kind of short story** the examiners want you to write about.

So now you need to ask yourself:

**Is there a climax in any of these stories, or a turning point where things change for at least one of the characters?**

This essay question turns out to be quite a good one, because you get three quite positive answers:

**In 'The Test' the climax comes when Marian finally loses her patience and snaps at the driving inspector, giving him the excuse to fail her.**

**In 'Death of a Spinster' the climax comes when the unscheduled car kills the main character.**

**In 'If I Quench Thee' the climax is when Stern murders Tod. This is also a turning point because Stern goes quickly from being in control of the situation to being arrested for murder.**

It's time to narrow down your choice. To help you do this, take another look at the words in the **second paragraph** of the task. This paragraph is where the examiners tell you **how** they actually want you to tackle the essay. The words of the second paragraph give you instructions that you must follow. If you don't obey the instructions in paragraph two of the task, you aren't answering the essay question and you will certainly not pass.

For this essay, these words in paragraph 2 are important.

Now you can narrow down your options by asking yourself:

**Are there any of the stories that don't really build up to the climax or turning point?**

In fact you could still write about two of the stories. In both of them the climax you have identified comes near, though not quite at, the end. In 'The Test' and 'If I Quench Thee' the events of the story lead up to and create the climax. In 'Death of a Spinster', however, the climax comes as a surprise after the carefully described details of the woman's dull life. This makes it not such a good story to write this essay about.

At this stage you can choose which essay to write by asking yourself:

**Which story do I know better?**

**Which one have I revised more carefully?**

**Which one do I think I could write about better?**

Or you could carry on looking through the relevant sections of the exam paper until you find a different essay that appeals to you even more.

## Now try this

Below you will see just the first paragraph from a number of essays taken from old exam papers. All of them could be used to get you to write about at least one of the stories or poems in this book. Some of them could fit more than one text.

For each one, decide which text or texts you could base the essay on. If you have studied other texts in class that are not included in this book, you can try to find essays to match those texts too.

1 Choose a novel or a short story in which you feel great sympathy for, or intense dislike of, one of the characters.

2 Choose a prose work of fiction or non-fiction which deals with an important human issue: for example injustice, or poverty, or scientific discovery, or religious belief, or any other issue which you regard as important.

3 Choose a character from a novel or a short story who seems to you to be unfortunate in life, or for whom the ending is unhappy.

4 Choose a poem which starts with a description of a small event or everyday incident but which then explores more serious issues.

5 Choose a poem in which a particular mood such as joy, anger or sorrow is created.

6 Choose a poem which successfully describes a person, or a place, or an animal.

7 Choose a poem which deals with an aspect of the less pleasant side of life.

8 Choose a poem in which a character or an incident or an experience is vividly described.

9 Choose a poem which makes you feel pity or sympathy for a person or an animal.

## Writing your introduction

The first paragraph you write in the essay will be your introduction. Whenever you write a literature essay, the same three things should appear in the introduction:

1 the title of the text you read

2 the name of the author

3 a clear indication of what you will be writing about.

As we've already seen, the first paragraph of the essay task helps you to choose which task you are going to do. Once you have chosen an essay to tackle, that same first paragraph of the task instructions is also useful for something else. It helps you to **write the introduction** to your essay. To do this, you are going to **recycle** many of the words from that paragraph.

Let's assume that you have chosen to do the essay task we looked at in detail earlier, and that you are going to write about 'The Test'. Here's the first paragraph from the essay task we saw earlier on. Look at the words printed in bold type.

You can recycle all of those words in the introduction of your essay. Those words help you to give a clear indication of what you will be writing about. You still need to add the title and author to these to have a complete introduction, which would end up looking like this:

Choose a novel
or a short story
in which there
is an obvious
climax or
turning point

*A short story in which there is an obvious climax is 'The Test' by Angelica Gibb.*

Can you see the words that have been recycled from the task instructions?

Now go back and look at the long list of opening paragraphs of essay tasks printed on the previous page. As it happens, the first paragraph on that list can also lead you into writing an essay about 'The Test'. That paragraph said this:

**Choose a novel or a short story in which you feel great sympathy for, or intense dislike of, one of the characters.**

So your introduction this time would look like this:

*One short story in which I feel great sympathy for one of the characters is 'The Test' by Angelica Gibb, in which I sympathise with the main character, Marian.*

Again, look for the words that have been recycled from the task instructions.

You should have noticed too that this time the pupil has had to add a little more information to the introduction, and has said which character she sympathises with.

## Now try this

That essay question also gave you the option of writing about a character you intensely dislike. Sticking to the same story, 'The Test', write an introduction to an essay which tackles that aspect of the question.

## Now try this

Look back at that whole list of opening paragraphs from essay instructions. Can you turn each one into the introduction to an essay? Every one of them suits at least one of the texts in this book.

## The summary paragraph

After the introduction, it's a good idea to write a **short** summary of your text. Any teacher can choose to teach his or her class any texts that they enjoy, and that they think their class will like. This means that you may end up writing your Critical Essay about a text that the exam marker has never read, or maybe never even heard of. Writing a **short** summary will give the marker a little bit of context and background, making it easier for him or her to understand comments you make about that text in your essay.

> ⚠️ **TAKE CARE!** You'll have noticed that bold type is used twice to remind you that you should be writing a **short** summary. The summary itself does not earn you any marks. It just helps you and the exam marker to get your heads clear. You must not waste precious exam time by waffling.

To let you see what I mean by a **short** summary, here's one for 'The Test':

> *In this story Marian takes her driving test. Despite being a skilled driver, she fails because of the test inspector's racist response to her as a black woman.*

That summary is just 28 words long. It should be easily possible to summarise most texts in fewer than 50 words.

## Now try this

Read the following summaries. They are both for texts you can read and study in this book. Which text is being summarised in each case?

1 In this story we follow an un-named woman through her routine life, seeing the opportunities she misses and the risks she fears. The story ends with her sudden death, and other people's reactions to this.

2 The poet describes his childhood experience of being bullied, and the sometimes surprising emotions this caused in him.

### Now try this

There are three more texts in this book that have not been summarised. Can you write summaries of those texts in 50 words or less? Or, if you have studied other literature texts in class, can you summarise those?

## The main body of your essay

Once you've written the introduction and summary, it's time for the main body of your essay. This main body will be made up of several paragraphs – four or five will be enough.

We've already looked very carefully at the fact that the first paragraph of the essay instructions tells you what sort of text to write about. The second paragraph of the essay instructions tells you **what you are actually going to do** in your essay. Remember, if you don't do what that second paragraph tells you to do then you aren't answering the question and you will not pass the essay. Here is the second paragraph of the essay question that we decided could suit 'The Test':

If you look at this instruction carefully, you will see that in this essay you have two main things to do:

1   **show how** the writer builds up to the turning point or climax

2   **say how** the turning point or climax is significant for the rest of the story.

In fact many of the Critical Essays you will find in past papers or in the exam give you two things to do.

## Now try this

You are going to see the first paragraphs of some essay instructions you have seen before. This time you will also see the second paragraphs of the instructions. From each second paragraph, pick out the two things you have to do in the main body of the essay.

Choose a novel or a short story in which you feel great sympathy for, or intense dislike of, one of the characters.

Briefly outline the situation in which the character finds himself or herself and show by what means you are made to feel sympathy or dislike.

Choose a prose work of fiction or non-fiction which deals with an important human issue: for example injustice, or poverty, or scientific discovery, or religious belief, or any other issue which you regard as important.

Identify and explain what the issue is and go on to describe the ways in which the writer has made the prose work thought provoking.

*I have to…*

*Then I have to…*

*I have to…*

*Then I have to…*

Choose a poem in which a particular mood such as joy, anger or sorrow is created.

State what the mood is and show how the poet has created it effectively for you.

Choose a poem in which a character or an incident or an experience is vividly described.

Briefly state what the poem is about and go on to say what techniques are used in the poem to catch and maintain your interest.

Choose a poem which makes you feel pity or sympathy for a person or an animal.

Show how both the content and the style of the poem create pity or sympathy.

*I have to…*

*Then I have to…*

*I have to…*

*Then I have to…*

*I have to…*

*Then I have to…*

Not every Critical Essay task gives you two things to do. For example, you may find one like this:

> **Choose a poem which successfully describes a person, or a place, or an animal.**
>
> **Show how the important features of the subject of the poem are illustrated in such a way as to make an impact on you.**

In this task you don't have two different things to do, you just have to look, in a proportionate way, at the important features of the person, place or animal being described. The important thing you must always do is read the question to find out clearly and exactly what you have to do and what you have to write about.

So, now that you know what you are supposed to do, how are you going to do it? Let's take another look at the second, instructing paragraph in the essay task that we thought would be good for 'The Test'. The words that tell you what to do have been picked out in bold.

> **Show how** the writer leads up to this turning point or climax, and **say what** is its significance for the rest of the story.

A good way to tackle this essay is to write a couple of paragraphs dealing with the first main thing, looking at how the story builds up to the turning point or climax. Then you could write two or three more paragraphs saying how this turning point or climax is significant for the rest of the story. As you write these paragraphs:

- every one of the main body paragraphs must help you to do what your chosen task tells you to do.
- every one of the main body paragraphs must use evidence from the text

## Now try this

Below is an example of a paragraph which does the two things mentioned above. Read it carefully and decide:

1 Does this paragraph come from the 'Show how . . . ' section of the essay or from the, 'Say what . . . ' section?

2 Which words in the paragraph show that this pupil is trying to stick to the chosen task?

3 Which words in the paragraph show the pupil is using evidence from the text?

The answers are at the end of the paragraph. Don't look until you have worked them out for yourself.

> One way that the story leads up to its climax, when Marian snaps at the inspector and fails the test, is that we can see her growing more tense. When the inspector expresses surprise that she can read well, Marian says:
>
> 'I got my college degree last year,'
>
> This is a clear statement of facts. Her actual words do not show strain, but the writer tells us:
>
> 'Her voice was not quite steady.'
>
> This tremor in her voice shows the pressure she is under. The writer is hinting to us that she may soon crack. Perhaps this is because by attacking her education, the inspector has picked on something which is extremely important to her.

Did you manage to answer the three questions?

1    This paragraph comes from the 'Show how . . .' section of the essay.

2    The words in the paragraph that show this pupil is trying to stick to the chosen task are:

**One way that the story builds up to its climax . . .**
**is that we can see . . .**

3    The words in the paragraph that show the pupil is using evidence from the text are:

**'I got my college degree last year,'**

and

**'Her voice was not quite steady.'**

Did you notice that this pupil once again recycled some words from the original essay question to help structure his paragraph? The words 'leads up to' are taken straight from the wording of the task.

Let's focus a bit more carefully on how to write the paragraphs in the main body of your essay. There are two things you should do in these paragraphs so that they will be well written and help you to achieve the task you've chosen.

1    You should begin the paragraph with a **topic sentence**

2    You should use the **ITQEE structure**.

## Topic sentences

**Topic sentences** are called this for two reasons:

- Firstly, they tie in with the topic of your essay.

- Secondly, they let the reader understand the topic of the paragraph you're on.

Using a topic sentence at the start of the paragraph sets you off in the right direction.

## Now try this

You're going to see again the five essay tasks you examined a few pages ago. After the tasks you'll see a list of sentences. Each one is a topic sentence from one of the five essays. Can you decide which essay each topic sentence belongs to?

Here are the essay topics:

1 Choose a novel or a short story in which you feel great sympathy for, or intense dislike of, one of the characters.

Briefly outline the situation in which the character finds himself for herself and show by what means you are made to feel sympathy or dislike.

2 Choose a prose work of fiction or non-fiction which deals with an important human issue: for example injustice, or poverty, or scientific discovery, or religious belief, or any other issue which you regard as important.

Identify and explain what the issue is and go on to describe the ways in which the writer has made the prose work thought provoking.

3 Choose a poem in which a particular mood such as joy, anger or sorrow is created.

State what the mood is and show how the poet has created it effectively for you.

4 Choose a poem in which a character or an incident or an experience is vividly described.

Briefly state what the poem is about and go on to say what techniques are used in the poem to catch and maintain your interest.

5 Choose a poem which makes you feel pity or sympathy for a person or an animal.

Show how both the content and the style of the poem create pity or sympathy.

Here are the topic sentences. Can you match each one to the right essay topic?

A The mood of anger is effectively created through the writer's use of the colour red.

B One way the author makes me feel intense dislike for Stern is by showing how critical he is about things that really matter to his daughter.

C An aspect of the writer's style is his use of similes.

D The writer makes the issue of loneliness thought-provoking by showing me that lonely people would sometimes rather be with other people who make them feel uncomfortable than be alone.

E A technique which allows the writer to describe the woman is the use of word choice connected to jewels and valuables.

## The ITQEE structure

**The ITQEE structure** helps you to remember what should be in each paragraph.

**IT** tells you to **I**ntroduce a **T**echnique. In other words, mention something you can see the writer deliberately doing.

**Q** tells you to give evidence by **Q**uoting from the text.

**EE** tells you to **E**xplain the **E**ffect of this, to show what the writer is doing to us, the readers.

The **IT** part of this is also the topic sentence of the paragraph, so there's a bit of an overlap between the idea of using a topic sentence, and the idea of following the ITQEE structure.

## Now try this

Copy out the paragraph below. Once you've copied it, do these three things:

1 underline the **IT** part with a straight line

2 underline the **Q** part with a wiggly or jagged line

3 draw a box round the **EE** part

*One way that the poet brings the woman vividly to life is by describing her clothes. She uses a mixture of positive and negative word choice to do so. Her coat, for example, is described as*

> *'drab plaid'*

*which makes it sound very unappealing. However her sari, peeping out beneath the coat, is described as having*

> *'gold embroidered gorgeousness'*

*The word 'gold' here makes the coat seem valuable and precious. 'Gorgeousness' is another very positive and praising word. Also, the alliteration of the g sounds at the start of these words draws our attention to the sari and makes us see how special and fascinating it is. The fact that the woman deliberately chooses to wear it despite the cold Glasgow weather tells me that it is important for this woman to stay in touch with and to celebrate her own culture, so her clothes tell us something about her personality too.*

Did you notice that the pupil placed his quotations so that they would stand out? They are **indented**, set in from the edges of the page to make it narrower than the rest of the essay. If you are quoting anything longer than just a single word or short phrase you should indent. It lets the marker see that you are using words from the text confidently.

You should also have spotted that the pupil is writing in **present tense**. You should do this whenever you write about what you have read.

## Now try this

Read the essay extract again. Pick out all the verbs which show that the pupil is writing in present tense.

# Writing about techniques

This is where the advice above each set of essay tasks comes in. The wording of this paragraph follows a pattern.

## Now try this

To get you to spot the pattern of this paragraph in the essay instructions, you're going to see the advice for two different types of essay. The first one is for **poetry** essays, the second one is for **prose** essays. Read the two paragraphs and then answer the two questions below.

Answers to questions in this section should refer to the text and such relevant features as: word choice, tone, imagery, structure, content, rhythm, theme, sound, ideas . . .

Answers to questions in this section should refer to the text and such relevant features as: characterisation, setting, language, key incident(s), structure, climax/turning point, plot, narrative technique, theme, ideas, description . . .

1 Which words are always used at the **start** of the advice above the essay tasks?

2 What do you always see at the **end** of the advice above the essay tasks? What do you think this means?

What this paragraph of advice does is just remind you to write about some of the techniques the author uses, or some of the things that made that text worth studying in the first place. Remember that **a technique is anything a writer deliberately chooses to do**. While some techniques have specific names, such as *simile, metaphor, alliteration* and so on, anything a writer does on purpose to have an effect on the reader is a technique.

It doesn't even actually matter which techniques and features you write about. You don't have to write about the ones named in the paragraph, because the three dots at the end of that paragraph allow you to write about whichever techniques and features you think are important for the text and task you have chosen.

For example, if you were writing an essay on 'The Test', and depending which essay you chose, you could pick any of the following techniques and features, which we looked at as we studied the story:

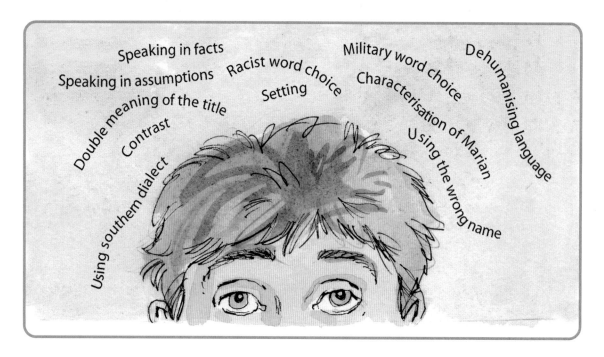

You don't necessarily have to force a technique into every one of your body paragraphs. It's still more important to make sure that every paragraph you write is tied into your chosen task and helps you to answer the question. You just have to pick up and deal with appropriate techniques on your way through the essay as you answer the question.

The way that you write about techniques is all tied in with that important **ITQEE** structure. The **IT** part, remember, is where you introduce the technique. The **Q** part is where you quote an example of that technique being used by the author. When you get to the **EE** part of the structure you explain how the writer creates an effect, or how the writer achieves what he or she set out to.

The following words and phrases describe **what the writer does**, or **what part of the text does**. They will help you to show that you are **analysing** the author's work.

| | | |
|---|---|---|
| **has connotations of** | **suggests** | **shows** |
| **creates**    **mirrors** | **establishes** | **underlines** |
| **reinforces** | **emphasises** | **highlights** |
| **foreshadows** | **exemplifies** | **explains** |
| **demonstrates** | **echoes**    **reveals** | **hints** |

The following words and phrases describe **how the reader feels**, or **how the text affects us** as we read. They will help you to show that you are **evaluating** the author's work.

| | | |
|---|---|---|
| thought-provoking | inspiring | horrifying |
| hard-hitting | stimulating | pivotal moment |
| key idea(s) | fast-paced | effective |
| gripping | skillful(ly) | perceptive |
| moving | profound | striking |
| important | intelligent | thoughtful |

## Now try this

You might want to work with a partner or group to do this. You should be quite familiar with this essay task by now. Can you think of:

- two more ways that 'The Test' builds up to the climax?
- two ways in which this climax is significant for the rest of the story?

Compare your answers with those from the rest of the class. Agree on the best two answers for building each main area of the essay.

## Now try this

Again, your teacher may let you work with a partner to do this. Look at the two ways and two reasons you agreed on above. Now turn each one into a paragraph for this essay.

Remember to:

- use quotations from the text and to indent the words that you quote
- make sure you start with a topic sentence and that that topic sentence works as the **IT** part of the **ITQEE** structure in your paragraph
- use some of the key words and phrases from the boxes above.

Read your paragraphs aloud in class or give them to your teacher for marking.

## The conclusion

After your introduction, summary and main body, you need to finish off your essay with a conclusion. The conclusion needs to do two things:

1    sum up and round off what you have written

2    give your personal response.

**Summing up** just means reminding the examiner what you have written about. It could be something like this:

*In this essay I have shown how the story 'The Test' builds up to a climax, and said what makes that climax significant for the rest of the story.*

**Giving your personal response** takes a little more thought. Earlier in your school career your personal responses were probably a bit like this:

*I liked the story because the writer made me feel sorry for Marian but I did not like the driving inspector because he was racist and unfair.*

You have to do something a little more complicated now, because at Intermediate 2 level your personal response, just like everything else in your essay, should fit your chosen task, as well as fitting the text you are writing about.

This task was about a climax, so your personal response should say something about what you thought of that climax when Marian snaps at the inspector and he fails her immediately. You could say whether you thought it seemed realistic, or how you felt about Marian behaving like that. Here's one example of how a pupil tackled it.

*The turning point is when Marian snaps at the inspector and he fails her immediately. This is an understandable thing for her to do, and I think it is very realistic. The author shows all the way through the story how much pressure Marian is under as the inspector attacks her background, her morals and her education. I understand that Marian probably cannot control herself any longer and he has simply pushed her too far. However I still wish she would not say what she does. She comes so close to passing her test, and then at the last minute she plays into the inspector's hands and lets him get away with failing her.*

So that's it. You know how to write an essay. If you've worked through this chapter you have found out step by step how to tackle this part of the exam. Before you go into the exam, your teacher will give you lots of chances to practise essay writing in class.

## Now try this

You're going to see the whole of the wording for that essay task on 'The Test' again.

First of all, above the essay choices for prose, the exam paper has this wording:

> Answers to questions in this section should refer to the text and such relevant features as: characterisation, setting, language, key incident(s), structure, climax/turning point, plot, narrative technique, theme, ideas, description . . .

Then you see this essay task:

> Choose a novel or a short story in which there is an obvious climax or turning point.

> Show how the writer leads up to this turning point or climax, and say what is its significance for the rest of the story.

Now, using all the advice from this chapter and everything you have learned, write this essay. Remember you need to have:

- an introduction

- a short summary

- about five main body paragraphs beginning with good topic sentences and using the **ITQEE** pattern

- a conclusion in which you summarise the essay and give your personal response.

Check over your essay and then hand it in to your teacher for marking.

At the end of the chapter about 'The Test' you will find other essay questions that fit that text. Every other literature chapter of this book also ends with a selection of essay questions you can try.

## Essay writing in the exam

During the Intermediate 2 course you will get lots of chances to write essays about the texts you study. At first your teacher may support you in some of the following ways

- giving you a plan to follow

- making a plan with the class

- letting you plan in groups or pairs

- letting you use your texts and notes while you write the essay

- giving you as long as you need to finish the essay

- letting you take the essay home to finish it.

However, by the time you get to the exam you need to be able to quickly choose, plan and write your essays, two of them, in 90 minutes.

Two things will help you with this.

**Firstly** you need to know your texts really well before you go in to the exam, and you need to know all your notes and materials about those texts. That way you can pick out the right material to use to answer the essay questions you have chosen.

Think of it like this. You probably have lots of clothes in your wardrobe. If you know what you've got, and you know what you're about to do, you can pick out the right outfit for the situation. The clothes you could choose to go camping wouldn't be the same ones you would choose to go to a party. The information you use to write an essay about how the author makes you feel sympathy for a character might not be the same information you would use to write an essay about how the writer deals with a particular theme or issue.

**Secondly**, you need to make a quick plan in the exam before you write each essay. It can be a list of the five key ideas you want to base your main body paragraphs on, or a spider plan with a leg for each main body paragraph, but however you do it you need to know what you are going to say to answer the question.

Sometimes, pupils go in to the exam and panic. No matter how scared you are, don't be tempted to write about the Film and TV Drama option if you haven't been taught that in class. Even if you are Scotland's biggest *Eastenders* fan, don't write about what you haven't been trained to write about. The same applies to the language section. There might well be a question in there about teenage slang, and you may be a slangy teenager, but don't try to write about it if you haven't been taught it.

Another danger in the exam is that you might write the essay you want to write, and not the one the examiners want. It's really important to learn essay skills – and that's what this whole chapter has been about – but there's no point trying to learn a particular essay off by heart, even if it's one you got a good mark for in class. You can only write about what the examiners want on that day.

Let's end with a piece of positive advice. If at all possible, you should try to make one of your two exam essays be about **poetry**. There's much less risk with poetry that you will fall into retelling the plot, which can sometimes happen with essays about novels or plays. Also, because poems are very short and the language in them has to work every hard, poems are stuffed with recognisable techniques. That it makes it very easy for you to identify these techniques and to write about them, which immediately makes your essays more analytical, and makes you seem more clever. Being short also makes poems easier to know, and easier to learn quotations from.

# The Personal Study

## What you have to do

The Personal Study is one of the four assessments, or NABs, that you have to pass in school. For this assessment you choose a literature text to study and then write an essay, the Personal Study, about it.

## What you are assessed on

Your teacher, who will assess your Personal Study, is actually looking at four different areas of your skill:

- **Understanding** What you write must show that you understand the main points of your chosen text. You should refer to parts of the text that are relevant to the topic you've chosen.

- **Analysis** You should examine the writer's structure, style and language. You need to show how these contribute to the meaning, effect and impact of the text you have studied.

- **Evaluation** You must show a personal response to the text you have read. This response should be supported by evidence.

- **Expression** The marker should be able to follow your line of thought through the Study. You should use spelling, grammar and punctuation well and clearly.

*I must ~~spel~~ spell and ~~punktu8~~ punctuate ~~properly~~ proply.*

# What makes this task challenging

The Personal Study is one of the most challenging tasks in this course because of the level of independence asked of you. You need to do all these things for yourself:

- choose a text

- read it in your own time

- make your own notes on the text

- work out what makes the text worth studying

- choose your own task and title

- plan the Study by yourself

- write and check over the Study for yourself before you hand it in.

That list above might sound very daunting. However if you think about it another way, the Personal Study is just another literature essay. If you wait until you've written a few Critical Essays in class before attempting your Personal Study, many of the things that make it seem hard will actually come quite naturally.

The Personal Study will follow the same pattern and structure that you are learning to use for other essays:

- There will be an introduction in which you name the author and title and explain what you will be writing about

- There will be a brief summary paragraph to give a flavour of the text

- The main body of the essay will have about four or five paragraphs that fit the task or title you have chosen.

- You will show that these paragraphs fit the task by starting each one with a good topic sentence.

- In those body paragraphs you will use the ITQEE structure.

- You will analyse the writer's style.

- Your Personal Study will end with a conclusion and personal response that fits your chosen task.

If all of that is familiar and makes sense, you're probably ready to have a go at your Personal Study.

## Choosing a text

### What to choose and what to avoid

You shouldn't write about a book you've ever studied in school. If you did this, it wouldn't be your own **Personal** Study.

You should choose a book where the writer is trying to create a good piece of literature as well as just tell a gripping story. Your teacher will be able to help you spot the difference.

You should almost certainly choose a book written for adult readers. Some books, such as *Northern Lights* and *The Curious Incident of the Dog in the Night-time*, have what's called 'crossover appeal' because adults have enjoyed them too. They are also both very well written, and have definite literary merit. In most case, however, a book written for younger readers will not give you enough to analyse.

Most examples of what we call **genre fiction** are unsuitable. These include most thrillers, most detective stories, most romances, most horror books and most of the books aimed at young woman readers and known as 'chick lit'. Writers of genre fiction tend to focus very much on plot. They often have quite simple themes and flat characters.

There are some examples of genre fiction that can be studied for this NAB. Although Stephen King is best known as a horror writer, **some** of his other works are appropriate. Also on that list is Ian Rankin, a Scottish writer whose books are about an Edinburgh detective called Inspector Rebus. Rankin's novels are very high quality and have lots you can examine.

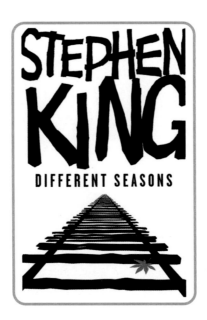

You also need to take care with books that tell real-life stories: biographies, autobiographies and memoirs.

These books are often interesting to read but poorly written. Someone who is famous for football or singing is unlikely to be a stylish writer too. Sometimes these people don't even write the story themselves. A paid author called a ghost writer may have written it for them, so the book is pretending to be something it isn't, and the author isn't really who you think it is.

Biographies of celebrities can be even worse. They may be written just to get money from fans, and are frequently made up of material from old interviews or news articles.

Some autobiographies and memoirs are well written. This tends to happen most when the book is about the life of someone who is not famous already, but has lived an unusual life. Even then, you have to be careful. You do get some autobiographies and memoirs by previously unknown writers which are still not worthy of study. In the last few years many top selling books have dealt with abusive childhoods – books like those by Dave Pelzer or Julie Gregory. They are gripping to read, but not stylishly written.

There's one more thing to take care about. If you do choose a well-written autobiography or memoir, you should steer clear of writing about the main character. When the main character is also the writer, it's hard for that person to be honest and objective about himself or herself. You can still choose a book like this, but it's better to stick to writing about something else like a theme, or an aspect of the writer's style.

So now that we've eliminated the books you shouldn't study, how will you find a good one?

## Where to get recommendations

Ask teachers, friends and family members about books they enjoyed and why. Staff at your local or school library will be able to help, especially if you explain why you need to choose a book and what you're going to do with it. Your teacher may take your whole class to a library. If you find a book that seems interesting your teacher should be able to let you know if it's suitable.

You could also make a shopping trip to somewhere like Waterstone's or Borders. These shops carry thousands of different books. Take time to browse and see what interests you.

You could also think about books you have previously enjoyed. You might want to try a new book by an author whose other work you have enjoyed or one that deals with a subject you find interesting.

When you pick a book up it's probably because you liked the cover, or the title, or because you recognised the name of the author. What should you do next?

- Read the blurb on the back. If it sounds interesting, go on to the next step. If not, put the book back and look for another one.

- Now open the book. Read the first couple of pages. If they seem interesting, go on to the next step. If not, put the book back and look for another one.

■ Sit down somewhere and read the first chapter, or the first ten pages. If you still like the book by this time, then it may well be the right book for you to study. If not, start again.

## Some suggestions

Below is just a brief list of some books that might be suitable for your Personal Study.

| Author and title | Summary | You might study . . . |
|---|---|---|
| ARNOTT, Jake<br><br>*The Long Firm* | Novel about a 1960s gangster, Harry Stark. Each chapter is told by a different character who knew him. | . . . Harry's character – is he just a violent bully or does he have a good side too? |
| ASHWORTH, Andrea<br><br>*Once in a House on Fire* | Ashworth describes how she and her mother and sisters coped with two violent stepfathers. | . . . the theme of violence, or how the book presents a particular view of what men are like |
| ATKINSON, Kate<br><br>*Behind the Scenes at the Museum* | Family story focusing on Ruby and her sisters. A surprising family secret is eventually revealed. | . . . the various ways the author hints at the secret, or the way that event affects family members |
| BANK, Melissa<br><br>*The Girls' Guide to Hunting and Fishing* | Jane's love life, from age 14 onward, is told in seven chapters. | . . . the different styles the writer uses for each of the chapters |
| BANKS, Iain<br><br>*The Crow Road* | Novel set in Glasgow. Prentice tries to find out why one of his uncles disappeared, and whether someone else in his family is responsible. | . . . relationships within Prentice's family |
| BANKS, Iain<br><br>*Espedair Street* | Daniel looks back on his time as a rock star, while trying not to let any of his friends know he used to be one. | . . . what it is that makes Daniel try to hide his past |
| BARKER, Pat<br><br>*Regeneration* | Novel set in the First World War, based on the real life of poet Wilfred Owen. | . . . the theme of war, or the different ways that war affects different characters |
| BROOKMYRE, Christopher<br><br>*A Big Boy Did it and Ran Away* | Funny and exciting Scottish novel about a teacher who ends up battling a terrorist. | . . . what makes the book quite different to most other thrillers |

| Author and title | Summary | You might study . . . |
|---|---|---|
| CADWALLADR, Carole<br><br>*The Family Tree* | We see Rebecca's life unfolding, and also follow her eccentric and unhappy childhood. | . . . what the author is saying about how our families shape who we are |
| DOHERTY, Berlie<br><br>*Dear Nobody* | Teenage pregnancy, told from the point of view of both young parents. | . . . the contrast between Chris and Helen, and how this is shown in the way they tell their stories |
| DOYLE, Roddy<br><br>*The Woman Who Walked into Doors* | Paula deals with her violent husband, her four children, and her own heavy drinking. | . . . Paula's character. How do her strengths and weaknesses help her to deal with her problems, or even cause them in the first place? |
| EDUGENIDES, Jeffrey<br><br>*The Virgin Suicides* | Novel about the five suicidal Lisbon sisters, narrated by the boys who loved them. | . . . what it is that makes the girls kill themselves, or you could look at the relationship between the girls and their parents |
| FIELDING, Helen<br><br>*Bridget Jones's Diary* | Single London girl records her attempts to find love and keep her weight down. | . . . Bridget – are we meant to relate to her or laugh at her? |
| FREUD, Esther<br><br>*Hideous Kinky* | The narrator and her sister get taken to live in Morocco by their hippy mother. | . . . how the writer makes the story seem to come from a child's point of view |
| GARLAND, Alex<br><br>*The Beach* | Richard finds his way to a backpackers' paradise in Thailand, but soon it all goes wrong. | . . . why the travellers' attempt to set up a perfect community goes wrong |
| GOLDING, William<br><br>*Lord of the Flies* | A group of schoolboys wrecked on a deserted island try to cope but end up trying to kill each other. | . . . the contrast between the two main characters, or the theme of the evil to be found in human nature |
| GREENE, Graham<br><br>*Brighton Rock* | Very young but brutal gangster, Pinky, terrorises 1950s Brighton. | . . . the character of Pinky, and what has made him so brutal so young |
| HADDON, Mark<br><br>*The Curious Incident of the Dog in the Night-time* | 15-year-old autistic Christopher solves a murder mystery and learns about his family and himself. | . . . how Christopher changes, or how he copes with challenges, or some of the features of the way he tells his story |

| Author and title | Summary | You might study . . . |
|---|---|---|
| HIGHSMITH, Patricia<br><br>*The Talented Mr. Ripley* | Charming con man kills a rich young man and takes over his life. | . . . Ripley's character – is he just a monster or does he have any redeeming features? |
| HILL, Susan<br><br>*I'm the King of the Castle* | Rivalry and violence between step brothers. | . . . the contrast between the two boys, or the ways their relationship develops and changes |
| HORNBY, Nick<br><br>*High Fidelity* | Record shop-owner Rob tries to get back together with his girlfriend and wonders why all his relationships go wrong. | . . . Rob's character, or how he relates to people, or what the author is trying to say about what modern men are like |
| KESEY, Ken<br><br>*One Flew Over the Cuckoo's Nest* | Residents of a mental hospital are disturbed by a new inmate, McMurphy. | . . .whether the residents are mad or whether the system and the nurse in charge are madder and more evil |
| LEE, Harper<br><br>*To Kill a Mockingbird* | Racism and prejudice in 1930s America, told from a child's point of view | . . . the theme of prejudice and misunderstanding, or you could examine one of the main characters |
| KING, Stephen<br><br>*The Shawshank Redemption* (this short novel is part of a longer book called *Different Seasons* | Andy spends nearly 30 years in prison, but is innocent and eventually escapes. | . . . Andy's character, or at how the prison environment brings out different qualities in different people |
| KRAKOUR, John<br><br>*Into Thin Air* | True story of a storm which killed many climbers on Everest. | . . . what the author is saying about the personality of those who climb huge mountains |
| McCourt, Frank<br><br>*Angela's Ashes* | McCourt describes his childhood of terrible poverty and hardship in 1930s Ireland. | . . . the theme of poverty and how it affects people, or the surprising amount of humour in the book |
| ORWELL, George<br><br>*Animal Farm* | Animals rise up against their master, but their fairer farm soon becomes just as unfair. | . . . what the writer is trying to say about humans and human society by using animal characters |

| Author and title | Summary | You might study . . . |
| --- | --- | --- |
| RANKIN, Ian<br><br>Inspector Rebus novels – you might want to try the first one, *Knots And Crosses*, or the best one, *Black and Blue* | Rebus solves crimes in Edinburgh, often in conflict with his colleagues and battling his own problems with drink, loneliness and broken relationships | . . . the character of Rebus – he's a very complex man with both good and bad qualities |
| SAKI<br><br>Short stories | Saki's stories were written early in the twentieth century. They are usually about rich and cultured people and they often have a twist in the tale. | . . . the writer's style, especially his use of twists, or you could look at whether he puts anyone in his stories that the reader can like or admire |
| SALINGER, J. D.<br><br>*The Catcher in the Rye* | Holden describes how being expelled from school led to a series of adventures in New York and eventual nervous breakdown. | . . . Holden's character, or his relationships with other people |
| SEBOLD, Alice<br><br>*The Lovely Bones* | Murder victim watches from Heaven as her family and friends deal with her death. | . . . the theme of grief and how different people react differently to it |
| SMITH, Dodie<br><br>*I Capture the Castle* | Cassandra and her eccentric family are broke and live in a half-ruined castle – will she and her sister Rose ever find love? | . . . the contrasting characters of Rose and Cassandra, or the different ways they deal with love |
| SPENCE, Alan<br><br>*Its Colours They Are Fine* | Collection of short stories about growing up in Glasgow in the 1960s. | . . . how the author handles important events in life, or how adult behaviour influences children, or you could just look at one or two stories and pick a suitable angle |
| SPARK, Muriel<br><br>*The Prime of Miss Jean Brodie* | Study of a school teacher and the influence she has on her pupils. | . . . is Miss Brodie a hero or a villain, a good influence or a bad one? |
| STEINBECK, John<br><br>*Of Mice and Men* | Two farm workers try to fulfil their dreams in 1930s America. | . . . the themes of loneliness, or hope, or the George–Lennie relationship |
| SWOFFORD, Anthony<br><br>*Jarhead* | American marine tells us about his time at war in Iraq | . . . the themes of violence and anger, and why these are still important even when there is no warfare going on |

| Author and title | Summary | You might study . . . |
|---|---|---|
| SYAL, Meera<br><br>*Anita and Me* | Meena, the only Indian child in town, becomes friends with, but eventually grows out of, the lively Anita. | . . . the theme of racism, or how Meena gradually begins to see what Anita is like, or the contrast between the two girls |

You have to choose a book that you like, because you'll be spending so long working on it. Discuss your choice with your teacher and make sure he or she agrees.

Once your choice is fixed, you should buy your own copy of the book. This means you can underline or highlight useful bits you'd like to quote from; you can write notes in the margin; you can turn back the corners of pages to remind you that that's where the important sections are.

# Choosing a title

Once you do have a suitable book, you need to work out your angle of study. To do this you need to get to know the book really well.

## Making basic notes

You may end up reading your chosen book more than once. The first time you read it you'll be doing so in a fairly general way. By the end of this reading you need a good outline of the text – what happens, who the characters are, how they relate to each other.

As you read right through the book for the first time you're going to do the following three things:

1  make notes after every five pages (or after every chapter if the chapters are very short) about what's happening

2  circle the name of each character the first time they are introduced

3  highlight or underline any important quotations you think you might want to use later – these might be things characters say, or parts of the story telling.

## Now try this

Take a look at the example below. A pupil is reading *The Family Tree* by Carole Cadwalladr, one of the books on the list of suggestions. Here are the pupil's written notes. This book has short chapters, so the pupil has made a note after every chapter.

*Ch 1.1 Rebecca describes the day in the 1970s when her family bought a caravan. She introduces her sister and mother, and also Alistair, her modern-day husband.*

*Ch 1.2 Rebecca remembers reading her uncle's unsuitable books with her cousin Lucy, and how the things she read about got her in trouble with her mother.*

*Ch 1.3 Rebecca explains how she met her husband Alistair.*

At the same time as making these written notes, the pupil also circled names of characters the first time they appeared, and underlined quotations she thought might be useful. Whenever she underlined a quotation she wrote in the margin of the book to remind herself why she thought the words might be useful.

## Now try this

Look at the first page of the novel. Can you see how the pupil marked the text?

# 1.1

*1   *How is the caravan connected to the idea of fate?*

*2   *Is she suggesting that something ended up going wrong after the photo was taken, something they couldn't predict?*

*3   *Does the blink mean her mother couldn't face the future? Or was her mother not actually happy?*

The Knowsley Clubman entered our lives like fate. Although from the outside, it looked like a caravan.   *1*

It appeared one morning in our driveway, an alien spaceship from a planet more exciting than our own. Inside, there was a Calor Gas stove with an eye level grill, and a fridge that was pretending to be a cupboard. Tiffany and I, experienced sniffers of nail varnish remover and petrol stations, stood on the threshold and inhaled the slightly toxic smell of new upholstery and expectation. I was eight years old and susceptible to the idea that technology could change your life. They said so in the TV ads.

I have a photograph from that day. We're standing in the driveway smiling, certain, shoulders locked together in a single row. It reminds me of one of those Soviet posters from the thirties: The Family Monroe, brave pioneers of a new type of *2* holiday, proudly facing the future together. The sun is making me squint, and my mother must have blinked because her eyes are *3* shut, but otherwise I'd say we looked happy.

## Now try this

It's time to read through your chosen text and write basic notes. Your teacher may wish to see these.

For the next step, you may need to read some parts of your book again. However you should be able to manage most of this by reading your basic notes and answering the following questions as you go.

## Now try this

Using your notes and your book, answer the following questions and follow the given instructions.

**Plot**

- In under 50 words, summarise the plot.
- Is it simple or complex?
- How original is it?

**Setting**

- When is the text set?
- How long does the story run from start to finish?
- Where is the text set?
- Is the setting unusual in any way, or is it ordinary?
- Do you think the setting matters to the story, or is it just a necessary background?

**Point of view**

- How is the story told? First person? Third person?
- If it's told in third person is this narrator omniscient (knowing everything) or does the narration still just follow the point of view of one character?
- How does this use of viewpoint affect us? Does it make us sympathise with, or believe, or dislike certain characters? Is it used to hide things from us?

**Structure**

How is the story organised? Is it:

- in order (chronologically)
- or jumping from one story to another (episodic)
- or building up to a climax
- or does it use suspense

- or does it use cliffhangers
- or does it use flashbacks
- or is it told using different forms of text (diary, letter)
- or is it based on solving a complication or problem that arises near the start of the book?

**Characterisation**

Now focus on the main character(s)

- Write about the kind of person/people they are, not just their appearance but more importantly their personality.
- How do they change or develop throughout the text?
- How do other people in the book react to or treat this/these character(s)?
- How does the writer use the character(s) to demonstrate the theme(s) of the book?
- How have you responded to this/these character(s)?

**Themes**

- What is/are the main theme(s) in this text?
- How does the writer put the theme(s) across?
- How well are themes put across?
- Has reading this text changed your attitudes or ideas?

**Style**

Here you are looking at HOW the text is written rather than what is being said.

- What is the strongest feature of the writer's style? Is it mainly descriptive; or mainly through dialogue; or driven by action; or full of the inner thoughts and feelings of characters?
- What sort(s) of language does the writer use? Is it formal; or colloquial; or complex; or descriptive; or trying to stir up the reader's emotions; or in dialect; or full of imagery?
- What is the writer's sentence structure like? Is it complex or simple?
- Does the writer use a lot of imagery? Give examples.
- Does the writer use symbolism, when an ordinary object has deeper meaning or stands for an important idea? Give examples
- Think about the writer's tone, his attitude to what is written about. It is humorous; or satirical; or bitter; or angry; or something else?

Your teacher may give you a date by which you should finish your notes, and will probably also ask you to hand these notes in for him or her to see.

## Finding an angle

Once you have your basic notes it's time to work out your **angle**. In other words you have to work out **what makes the book worth studying**.

When we study a text, most of what we might analyse fits into the following five areas.

- **Plot** – what happens in the text, in the order it happens

- **Character** – the people in the text, usually focusing on main or important or interesting characters

- **Setting** – where and/or when the text happens

- **Theme** – the ideas the author is trying to explore, the issues he or she wants readers to think about or learn about

- **Style** – any particular features or techniques that the writer deliberately uses in the text.

So let's use those headings and some questions that go with them, to help you narrow down your angle of study.

## Now try this

You will need a photocopy of the following three pages. For each of the five areas listed above you'll find a few questions. First of all, read back over the notes you made about your book. Then answer the questions by filling in the boxes on your photocopy.

You should try to answer each question, *but* you might not end up with an answer for every one.

Name:_____ Class:_____

Does the writer use any of the following **plot** techniques? Tick if you found:

A **flashback**, when we are taken suddenly back to earlier events ☐

A **turning point**, after which everything is different for the characters, or the story goes off in a different mood or direction ☐

A **twist or shock**, when something really unexpected happens ☐

A **climax** which the story builds up to, perhaps where the action becomes very dramatic, angry or even violent ☐

A plot that is **episodic**, jumping from one little story to another rather than having telling a single long story throughout ☐

If you have ticked any of the boxes above, use the next box to make brief notes about what it was you found interesting.

Who was the main **character** in your text?

Describe that person, especially their personality, by using a few key phrases.

Does this person change, grow, or develop over the course of the text? If so, how? Does he or she learn a lesson? If so what?

Name:_____ Class:_____

Was there another character you found particularly interesting? Who was it, and why were you interested?

Is there an important relationship, or important conflict between two (or more) characters in this text? If so, outline it briefly.

Does the text have a **setting** that is especially well-described or brought to life? If so, what is it? What makes the description so good?

Does the setting affect or change the characters or the plot? If so, how?

Can you identify one or two important **themes** in this text? What is it?/What are they?

How does the author mainly show this/these theme(s)?

Name:_____ Class:_____

Does the writer use any of these **aspects of style**? Tick if you found any of these:

Humour ☐

Similes, metaphors or other images ☐

Deliberately breaking any of the usual rules ☐

Creating a particular point of view ☐

Using hints, or only gradually revealing something ☐

Contrast ☐

Using lots of slang, or swearing, or special jargon ☐

Did you notice anything else in the writer's style that seemed to be deliberate or special? If so, what?

[ ]

Did you notice anything else about the text that seemed to be important?

[ ]

You should be much closer now to working out what makes the book worth studying.

## Now try this

Read back over what you have written in all the boxes. You may also want to re-read your book notes one more time. Then answer the two questions below:

1 Which aspect of this book would you like to write about in your Personal Study?

2 Which aspect(s) of the writer's style and language will you particularly concentrate on?

## Turning the angle into a title

Your title should show right away that you are going to be really studying and analysing your text, not just writing about it. The biggest danger you face is that you might just end up rehashing the plot.

You have already done a great deal to avoid that danger, because your second set of notes and your answers to the three pages of questions have helped you to find out what makes your chosen text worth studying. The next thing you can do to help yourself is to create a title that shows that your work is analytical.

There are three things you should put in the title:

1 the name of the text

2 the name of the author

3 the aspect of the text which you have chosen to study

It's also a really good idea to begin your title with the words:

**A study of how (NAME OF AUTHOR) . . .**

or

**A study of (NAME OF AUTHOR)'s . . .**

That way you are making it clear from the outset that you are studying the text, and looking at the author's skills and techniques.

To make that clear, let's go back to the pupil working on the novel *The Family Tree,* which was listed earlier in the chapter. We've already seen how she began her notes about the book and looked at her text marking on the first page of the book. Here's her title:

## Now try this

You are going to see a list of Personal Study titles. They are all based on novels from the list of suggestions earlier in the chapter. Read the titles. Decide for each of them whether the pupil is concentrating on plot, character, setting, theme, or some particular aspect of the writer's chosen style.

1   A study of how Iain Banks explores family relationships in the novel *The Crow Road*

2   A study of how Jake Arnott depicts Harry Stark in the novel *The Long Firm*

3   A study of how Kate Atkinson gradually reveals the family secret in the novel *Behind The Scenes at the Museum*

4   A study of Melissa Bank's different styles for each chapter in the novel *The Girl's Guide to Hunting and Fishing*

5   A study of how Pat Barker shows the ways war affects different people in the novel *Regeneration*

6   A study of how Christopher Brookmyre breaks the usual rules of thriller writing in the novel *A Big Boy Did it and Ran Away*

7   A study of how Harper Lee shows different forms of prejudice in the novel *To Kill a Mockingbird*

8   A study of how the author creates an oppressive environment in the novel *The Virgin Suicides* by Jeffrey Eugenides.

9  A study of how we are made to both like and laugh at the main character in the novel *Bridget Jones Diary* by Helen Fielding.

10 A study of how Ian Rankin depicts Inspector Rebus in the novel *Black and Blue*

11 A study of how Holden Caulfield relates to the different people he meets in J.D. Salinger's novel *Catcher in the Rye*

12 A study of how Dodie Smith contrasts Rose and Cassandra in the novel *I Capture the Castle*

13 A study of how Muriel Spark shows Miss Brodie's good and bad sides in the novel The *Prime of Miss Jean Brodie*

14 A study of how the author uses the supposedly perfect community to explore human nature in the novel *The Beach* by Alex Garland.

15 A study of how the way Christopher narrates the novel *The Curious Incident of the Dog in the Night Time* by Mark Haddon gives us an insight into his mental condition.

16 A study of Paula's strengths and weaknesses in the novel *The Woman Who Walked into Doors* by Roddy Doyle.

17 A study of how William Golding uses contrast to explore human nature in the novel *Lord of the Flies*

18 A study of the relationship and conflict between the two boys in the novel *I'm the King of the Castle* by Susan Hill

19 A study of the theme of violence in the memoir *Once in a House on Fire* by Andrea Ashworth

20 A study of violence, anger and aggression in the memoir *Jarhead* by Anthony Swofford

## Now try this

You've read your novel and made notes. You've answered questions to help you narrow down your angle. You've seen how to construct a title and read 20 example titles. Now write the title for your Personal Study.

Give a note of your chosen title to your teacher. You shouldn't move on to the next stage until he or she agrees you have made a good choice.

# Planning your Personal Study

You should not write your Personal Study until you have written at least a couple of literature essays in class. You need to be familiar with the structure for an essay, and with how to build paragraphs using the ITQEE technique.

All of that is covered in a different chapter of this book, so we are not going to say too much here about planning and writing your Study.

Whatever your Study is about, at this stage you need to build yourself quite a detailed plan, fleshed out with notes and quotations.

## Using ITQEE to plan your study

Remember that:

**IT** tells you to introduce a technique

**Q** tells you to give evidence from the text by quoting

**EE** tells you to explain the effect of this, to show what the writer is doing to us.

If you are going to use the **ITQEE** structure to plan your Study, you should write the **IT** section as a complete sentence. That's because whatever you write in the **IT** section will end up being used as the **topic sentence** of a paragraph. Remember, these are called topic sentences for two reasons. Firstly, they tie in with the topic of your essay.

Secondly, they let the reader understand the topic of the paragraph you're writing.

For a Personal Study with the following title:

> **A study of how the author uses the supposedly perfect community to explore human nature in the novel *The Beach* by Alex Garland**

the ITQEE plan might read as follows:

| IT | Q | EE |
|---|---|---|
| Garland shows us that Richard is extremely excited and positive when he first reaches the beach community. | 'The height of the tree alone was breathtaking' . . . ''Camouflage,' said Jed behind me. 'We don't want to seen from the air. Planes fly over sometimes.' p. 88 | He's so amazed by the surroundings that he doesn't notice they are used to protect the community from a threat. We see that the community isn't perfect, but he's too excited to notice. |
| The author uses references to the Vietnam war. | 'Fragging. Blagging. Klicks. Grunts. Gooks. Charlie.' p. 100 | These references begin as soon as Richard reaches the beach, and hint at the violence to come. |

Just in case you're planning to write that Study, the example only has a couple of rows filled in. You should be able to fill about three more rows, using this as a pattern. Altogether you need about five rows in your table, so that you are planning for about five paragraphs in the main body of your Study.

## Now try this

It's time to plan the main body of your study. Whichever way you do it, you need to have a plan that will give the Study about five main body paragraphs.

Take a blank piece of paper, write your chosen title at the top, and plan your Study now.

## Now try this

Once you've written your plan, read it over. Ask yourself:

- Do I have **four or five clear points** to make?

- Is the first column of my plan all written in **whole, topic sentences**?

- Does my plan show that I am really going to **analyse** my text, and look at the writer's skills and techniques?

Your teacher may wish to see the plan when it's finished.

## The introduction and summary

You should already have written at least a couple of literature essays in class. This means that you should be quite confident about writing essay introductions, and that it should be easy for you to write a short summary of your chosen text. Remember you can also look again at the chapter of this book about literature essays.

However, just to save you flipping backwards and forwards through this book, here's a quick reminder:

The following three things should appear in the introduction:

1  the title of the text you read

2  the name of the author who wrote this text

3  a clear indication of what you will be writing about.

After the introduction, it's a good idea to write a **short** summary of your text. This summary will give your teacher a little bit of context and background, making it easier for him or her to understand comments you make about your chosen text. Remember to keep it brief.

The introduction and summary might be two very short paragraphs, or you might find that what you want to say fits together better in one slightly longer one. Whatever you write should very closely fit your chosen task and title.

Have a look at this example. Here's the task this pupil has chosen:

> A study of how William Golding uses contrast to explore human nature in the novel *Lord Of The Flies*

This is how this pupil's introduction and summary turned out:

> *William Golding's* <u>Lord of the Flies</u> *tells the story of a group of English schoolboys whose plane crashes on a deserted island. Their attempts at creating a fair and safe society soon go wrong, and island life descends towards violence and murder. Showing this decline allows Golding to display his view of human nature, and this is emphasised by the contrast between the two main characters, Ralph and Jack.*

You've just seen an example of a good introduction and summary. Now you're going to see a bad one. The pupil has chosen this title for her study:

> A study of how the way Christopher narrates the novel *The Curious Incident of the Dog in the Night-time* by Mark Haddon gives us an insight into his mental condition

So far, so good. However, this is the way the pupil's Personal Study begins:

> *Christopher is fifteen and he has Asperger's Syndrome. At the start of the story he finds his neighbour's dog dead in the garden and he starts to investigate this crime. As the book goes on he learns all sorts of secret things about his family, especially about what happened to his mum who he thinks is dead and about what his dad, who he usually trusts, is really like. He ends up going on a journey to London which is a big step for him because he has never left his hometown before. The whole story is told from his point of view and the way he tells us the story lets us see how his mind works like he has to tell us exactly what other people say to him or he can tell us little tiny details of things that he has seen. Sometimes he even uses swearing because that is what people have said to him and he just tells us about it. At the end of the book his family is different and we have learned much more about what life is like if you have Asperger's.*

This opening has far too much plot, and it misses out some of the things that should appear at the start of any essay.

**Now try this**

Can you rewrite the above opening and make it better?

## The conclusion

There's just one more thing you need to think about before you can actually write your Personal Study. You need to decide what you want to say in your conclusion.

You should know from your essay writing experience so far that you have to do two things:

1  sum up and round off what you have written

2  give your personal response.

Summing up just means reminding the marker (your teacher) what you have written about. Giving your personal response takes a little more thought. Your personal response, just like everything else in your essay, should fit your chosen task, as well as fitting the text you are writing about. There's more about this in the chapter on how to write a literature essay.

**Now try this**

Even though you haven't yet written your whole essay, you should already be able to write your conclusion. After all, you know your text very well and you have a very detailed essay plan, which means you actually know the material for you essay very well too. Write your conclusion now. Your teacher may wish to see it.

## Writing your Personal Study

### Controlled conditions

Writing your piece has to be done under what are called **controlled conditions**. This means that you will work in class, but under exam conditions. You'll have to be well prepared for this.

You can use your copy of the text, which should be marked up with highlights, underlining and notes. You can use your plan for the body paragraphs, and also the introduction, summary and conclusion you have written already. You won't be allowed to use a dictionary or thesaurus. You will have about an hour for your writing.

## What to do

First of all, neatly write out your introduction and summary. Then, following your plan, write the main body of the essay. This should consist of about four or five paragraphs. Each should follow the ITQEE structure and should begin with one of the topic sentences you wrote. Finish your essay by adding the conclusion you prepared already.

## Now try this

When you've finished, read your work over before you hand it in to your teacher. Think about the four areas you will be assessed on and ask yourself the following questions:

**Understanding**
- Have I shown that I understand my chosen text?
- Have I referred to the text to back up the points I make?

**Analysis**
- Have I analysed **how** the writer writes, and not just retold the story?

**Evaluation**
- Have I shown my personal response?
- Have I given evidence to show why I responded this way?

**Expression**
- Are my spelling, grammar and punctuation good?
- Is my point of view clear?

## What happens next?

Your teacher will now spend some time reading and marking your Personal Study. If your Study is written well enough then you will have passed.

If you have not passed, your teacher should give you some advice, either in writing or in person, to explain how your Study can be improved. You do not need to start again with a new book. You should only need to re-write parts of your Study. Make sure you understand what you have to do to be able to pass second time round – you won't be able to ask once you start re-writing.

# The Writing NAB

One of the four assessments, or NABs, that you have to pass in school before the exam is to produce your own piece of original writing.

## What the markers are looking for

When your work is marked, your teacher is looking at four different areas of your writing skill: **content, structure, expression** and **technical accuracy**.

- Your **content** should be relevant to the writing task you are doing. It should be suitable for the audience who will read it. You should develop a number of different points or ideas.

- Your piece should have good **structure**. It should be organised, straightforward and clear to follow. The structure should suit your chosen task and suit the likely audience who will read what you write.

- In your **expression** you should use the techniques we expect to find in your chosen genre of writing. You will find guidelines in this chapter about two particular genres of writing. You need to choose suitable words and vary the types of sentences you use. The reader should be able to recognise your point of view in what you write.

- **Technical accuracy** is how well you use the English language in your writing. This includes your spelling, grammar and punctuation, which should all be accurate.

Your final piece of writing has to pass in **all four** of these areas.

If you don't pass first time you will receive feedback about your work and have the opportunity to try again.

## Working conditions

You will have time in class to learn about the particular writing skills needed. You should get a chance to discuss what you are going to write about, and to make a plan.

When you eventually write your piece this has to be done under what are called **controlled conditions**. This means that you will have to work on your own, in class but under exam conditions. You will have about an hour to write your piece of work. This may all sound tough, but remember this comes after lots of preparation time.

## Different types of writing

There are several different genres, or types of writing, which you can choose for this NAB. Many options are open to you, but in this book we are going to concentrate on just two of them: Personal Reflective Writing and the kind of writing in which you handle ideas and opinions.

## Personal Reflective Writing

You are most likely to do really well in the essay writing NAB if you choose to produce a piece of Personal Reflective Writing. Why do you think this is?

### Now try this

Work with a partner, a small group, or with your class. Make a list of all the reasons you can think of to explain why people do best at this type of writing.

## Choosing what to write about

It shouldn't be too hard for you to choose a topic. After all, you know yourself better than anyone else does. Only you have lived your life. You are the only person in the world who has had your particular set of experiences. You are the only person in history who ever had the exact set of family and friends that you have. Your brain is the only one in the entire universe to hold your set of memories, thoughts and feelings. You are unique, interesting and well worth writing about.

## Now try this

Stop and think. Is there an experience you have had which matters to you very much, one that you'd like to write about in your Personal Reflective essay? If there is, write it down now and keep that note.

### Narrowing down your ideas

If you don't already have a subject in mind, then it may help you to think very quickly about a lot of different experiences you may have had, to see if any of them are suitable for a longer piece.

### Now try this

Can you write just one paragraph for each option below?

- What is the worst thing that has ever happened to you?
- What is the hardest thing that has ever happened to you?
- What is the happiest thing that has ever happened to you?
- What is the saddest thing that has ever happened to you?
- What is the most frightening thing that has ever happened to you?
- What is the strangest thing that has ever happened to you?

### Now try this

Can you write just one paragraph for each of these options below?

Which event or time in your life:

- has most shaped you
- has made you grow up or mature
- has most changed your family
- has been most confusing
- showed you the best of people/someone
- showed you the worst of people/someone?

### Now try this

Now you are going to think about some ways a person could make an impact on your life. Again, can you write just one paragraph for each option below?

Which person:

- has most influenced you
- has most helped you
- has most hurt you
- do you miss most
- are you most glad to be rid of?

## Now try this

You should now have up to seventeen short paragraphs in front of you. Read them over. Is there one you could write about in depth in your Personal Reflective essay? If there is, write it down now and put your note somewhere safe.

## Some possible tasks

If that still hasn't given you an idea, you'll see a list of tasks below. In each one, the main thing you have to write about is printed in bold. The following advice in plain type is to help you plan your writing. It will remind you about the thoughts, feelings, details, description and reflection that you need to use throughout.

- **Write about a relationship that has changed greatly, either for the worse or for the better.** If it is relevant, explain how the relationship first began. Make clear what the relationship was like before the change, and what caused that change. What is the relationship like now? Do you think it might change again in the future? Use thoughts and feelings throughout. Reflect on what you have learned about yourself, and about the other person (or people) involved.

- **Write about a time when you felt isolated.** Explain the circumstances that led you to feel this way, how you handled the experience at the time and how it has gone on to affect you.

- **Write about a time when you were in conflict with someone over a particular issue.** Be sure to include your thoughts and feelings at the time. Reflect on how that conflict has affected you and how you feel about it now.

- **Write about a time when you lost someone or something special.** Deal with your thoughts and feelings at the time of the loss. Make it clear how you felt then and why. Through reflection, show how you feel now about this loss.

- **Write about a time when you experienced personal success.** Concentrate on your thoughts and feelings at the time. Make sure you reflect on how that success has changed or affected you.

- **Write about a time when you were given some responsibility.** Write about how you carried that out at the time and show what you thought and felt. Did you handle that responsibility well or badly? Reflect on what you learned or gained from having this responsibility.

# Good writing techniques

## Thoughts and feelings

Your Personal Reflective Writing will really come to life when you include your thoughts and feelings. No one else knows these. Only you can tell the reader about them.

To show you what I mean, let's look at an example.

The writer Patrick Woodhead was part of a team planning to ski to the South Pole. On a training trip, bad weather stopped them from making any progress.

The weather was completely shut in and there was no chance of going further up the hill. We had been eating huge meals to stock up before we went to the mountain, and this further setback meant we all had way too much energy. The ominous black clouds made the air feel heavy and oppressive and did little to alleviate our pent-up angst.

For four days we hung around that tiny village at the base of the Fox Glacier waiting for a break in the weather. It was so incredibly frustrating to wake up each morning to see the blanket of clouds and the helicopters locked firmly in the hangar. We would be leaving for Antarctica in just a couple of months and yet here was our training slowly being squandered by endless weather delays. This was the time when we should have been testing ourselves, our equipment, and more importantly finding out whether we could work effectively as a team. I just had no idea whether I was capable of skiing to the pole, and having the days slip away from me while we sat morosely in our little hotel did little to relieve my doubts.

When cabin fever started to set in I decided to go for a run. I set off for a beach about ten kilometres away.

After following winding forest trails I came down to a place called Gillespie Beach and looked upon the most glorious stretch of coastline I have ever seen. The scene looked prehistoric, like something out of The Land That Time Forgot, and it felt incredible to see somewhere so untouched.

It was wonderful to see somewhere so spectacularly beautiful, with life and colour as vivid as I could remember.

Standing, looking out to sea, I realise this was the first time I had felt properly relaxed in weeks. I had been feeling tetchy of late, and had found myself having to bite my tongue on a couple of occasions to stop myself snapping at the others. I wasn't sure why. Possibly it was the oppressive black cloud back at Fox village or some subliminal apprehension I was feeling about leaving for Antarctica.

## Now try this

Woodhead is obviously feeling a mixture of emotions, some positive, some negative. Copy and complete the following table to help you explore the emotions in the extract.

| Emotion | Evidence | Positive or negative? |
|---------|----------|----------------------|
| self-doubt | 'I just had no idea whether I was capable of skiing to the Pole.' | negative |

Interestingly, people often write extremely well about hard experiences. If we go through sad, difficult or tragic events we are strongly aware of how we feel at the time. Sad events affect and shape us. We have to keep working with and processing the memories, thoughts and feelings that go with these events.

## Details and descriptions

Because your memories are important to you, when you bring them to mind they will be full of tiny details, things you noticed at the time. Many of these details might not be very important in themselves, but they become important because they bring that memory to life.

To let you see what I mean, here's a piece in which Nigel Slater remembers his childhood.

The most forbidden of places was my father's bedside drawer. I had never been told not to go there; I just knew it was out of bounds. A secret place. An ivory coloured drawer set in a glossy black table, gold handle, its perfect patina interrupted only by a ring burned in the top by a hot mug. My mother's, on the other hand, was an open book. A jumble of tissues and hairpins, powder compacts and sweets. Home to one of the many Ventolin inhalers tucked discreetly around the house.

His drawer was neat, and smelled of the cortisone cream he smoothed into his hands in the autumn when each year a weird rash would flare up. There were several opened tubes of Setlers. There were several menus of dinners he had been to, often with the signatures of those who had attended inside.

Setlers were as much a part of my dad's DNA as his pipe and his Daily Telegraph. The chalky white tablets went everywhere with him; half and quarter packets were in every jacket pocket, including the one in his suede waistcoat, and in the glove box of the car. Ten times a day he would rub his sternum and tear another strip of wrapper off his indigestion pills.

This short passage is stuffed with tiny details. We know exactly what each of Nigel Slater's parents kept in their bedside drawers, and what one of the table tops looked like. We know all about his father's addiction to indigestion tablets.

## Now try this

Read the following extract from Chris Stewart's book *The Almond Blossom Appreciation Society*. As you read it, make a list of the small details which make it seem vivid and convincing.

At the beginning of the year, my daughter Chloe and I decided that we had to get fit, and that the best way to do this would be to create a running track in the riverbed. We go there every evening now and our pounding feet have marked out a fairly clear circuit.

The grass is long and makes a pleasant thripping noise as you race along, and in spring the ground is sprinkled with dandelions and daisies which grow so dense that, through half-shut eyes, you might be running though a field of cream. The track, however, remains just a bit too rustic for a good sprint. You have to be careful to hop over the thistles, skip to avoid an ankle-cracker of a stone, and cut close to the broom bush on the third turn while ducking to avoid a poke in the eye. The second turn is between the third and fourth euphorbia bushes and the start and finish is at the tamarisk tree where we hang our sweaters. The going is soft sandy turf.

As we returned from our run the other night Chloe called me excitedly to the gate. I turned back and looked where she was pointing. There, battling its way across the track was a dung beetle.

This particular beetle had lost its jet-black shine under a thick covering of dust. It was steering a ball of dung with its back legs, while it scrabbled for purchase with its horny front legs. Progress was unthinkably difficult as the ground was rough, and of course it was quite unable to see where it was going, head down, facing away from the desired direction of travel. The ball kept going out of control and rolling over the poor creature, yet without so much as a moment to dust itself down, the beetle picked itself up and patiently resumed rolling on its intended course.

## Using dialogue

One more thing you can do to bring your writing to life is to put speech into it. If you can't remember the exact words you and other people said, you can make up something which sounds like what you remember.

Here is Andrew Collins writing about when he was a student in London, and went to see a flat he and his friend Rob were interested in renting.

There was no sign of Mr. Rabbit outside at the pre- arranged time. We rang the bell. No answer. Then we heard a disembodied posh voice.

'Are you looking for Claire?'

Rob and I stepped back from the door into the apology for a front garden and craned our necks. A dark-haired woman had her head out of the window on the top floor.

'No, we've come to see Flat 2.'

'Oh. OK.' She put her head back in and closed the window.

Then a light came on in the hall and the front door opened. A girl who looked like she had hauled herself out of her sickbed was standing at the crack in the front door.

Rob went forward. 'We're supposed to be meeting Mr. Rabbit?'

'Rabeet.' She said his name the way the poor of Nottingham in Robin Hood's time must have uttered the name of the sheriff. 'You can come in if you like.'

She introduced us to a second pallid girl. They were student nurses. They didn't exactly sell the place.

'You've got access to the garden, but it's so overgrown we've never been out there to be honest.'

'What's the central heating like?'

The nurse gave a rueful but not unkind snort. 'There are gas fires in both fireplaces. Bit dodgy, but we leave them on all evening.'

'That sounds a bit pricey,' said Rob through a sharp intake of breath, the very picture of his own dad as usual.

'It's the only way to warm the place up.'

## Now try this

Just to show why the version with dialogue is better, try to rewrite this piece so that we get all the same information, but without any of the characters speaking.

### Being reflective

So far, in looking at using thoughts, feelings, details, descriptions and dialogue, we have been concentrating on the basic skills of Personal Writing. However this task is called Personal **Reflective** Writing. To be able to pass, you need to write **reflectively**. This is something that only mature and insightful writers are able to do.

This means two things at once.

If you stand in front of a mirror you can examine yourself pretty thoroughly by looking at your reflection. Every spot and blemish will be visible, but you'll also be able to see all your good features and everything that you like about yourself.

That's the first meaning of being reflective in Writing – **examining yourself**. You might question and criticise yourself. On the other hand you might realise that you handled the situation well. You may realise that certain experiences have shaped you and made you into the person you are, just as growing up changes the way your face looks in the mirror.

Now think of the rear view mirror in a car. The driver can keep his or her eyes on the road ahead, while using the mirror to see what is happening behind.

That's the second meaning of reflection: **looking back**. Often events in our lives make much more sense once they are over and we are older and wiser. Perhaps when something happened to you it was a really terrible experience, but now you realise that you benefited from it in some way. Events may be confusing when they happen, but when you look back on them they may make more sense.

As well as reflecting on yourself you can reflect on others. It may be that you disagreed with someone at the time, but you now realise they did the right thing. On the other hand, when we are young we sometimes accept the things adults do without question, but as we grow up we are not so sure about their motives. You may also be aware of how events and experiences have affected other people as well as yourself.

You can even make your reflection go wider still, showing that your experiences have taught you something about life, about society, or about people in general.

Below is a list of reflective phrases. Any of these phrases can be used to begin a reflective sentence or a reflective paragraph. In fact if you use one of them, whatever you write in the rest of the paragraph will definitely be reflective.

| | |
|---|---|
| Looking back . . . | Because of this I am . . . |
| On reflection . . . | Since this happened I . . . |
| With hindsight . . . | When I think back on this . . . |
| In retrospect . . . | Thinking about it now I feel . . . |
| Nowadays I feel/think/believe . . . | At the time I . . . but now I . . . |
| If I could do this again . . . | If I could change things . . . |
| If this happened now . . . | It was a . . . thing to do because . . |
| I learned . . . | I wish this had never happened because . . . |
| I realise . . . | Now that I've been through this . . . |
| I understand . . . | I grew through this experience because . . . |
| I should have . . . | This made me think about . . . |
| I could have . . . | This experience shaped me by . . . |
| I wish I had . . . | I'm glad this happened because . . . |

## Looking at some real examples

You are going to see two pieces of Personal Reflective Writing produced by real pupils

### Now try this

First of all just read through the two pieces of writing. You may wish to do this aloud around the class, or you might want to read them on your own.

A vivid memory I have is of a certain day when I babysat for my cousins. The older one, Katie, was at Brownies painting plant pots, leaving me and five year old Connor to play a game until she returned.

When I arrived I was greeted on the doorstep by a shy little Peter Pan. Connor was dressed in one of the many fantastic costumes he owns. He keeps them in a wooden box which sits against the wall that his dad painted for him four years ago. A huge space ship with blue and orange flames appears to have just blasted off from the lid of the box. Connor loves it. It is one of the few possessions he has to remind him of his dad.

Sometimes I've even tried to fit in to one of the 'baddie' costumes so we can have a play fight. Needless to say, I've always failed. I don't think a five-year-old's dressing up box is meant to cater for a fifteen-year-old girl.

As I smiled warmly at Connor in his costume he declared, 'You have been taken prisoner!'

I giggled to myself and thought, 'This will be interesting.' Little did I realise that I was going to spend the next half hour tied up with a skipping rope and trying to avoid the plastic toys being hurled at high speed towards me.

'Stop! Aargh!' I yelled, as a Ninja Turtle narrowly missed poking my eye out.

The distress in my voice must have been obvious. Connor stopped lobbing dangerous objects and insisted quietly, 'They are cannonballs!'

Nevertheless I managed to untie myself and get Connor to help me tidy up. I wrestled him into a fireman's lift and he squealed and wriggled as I carried him up the stairs, threatening to tickle him if he didn't get straight into his pyjamas.

This was actually a fairly easy task as over the month or two since I had started babysitting the children had learned to get changed when I told them to. In fact they are always very well behaved when I look after them.

Nowadays I feel much closer to them than before I began babysitting, and I still grow fonder of them every day. Looking after them is a good thing for me to do, as it helps my auntie when she has to go out without them. There really is no one else who can help.

Occasionally Connor and Katie will mention their dad in passing conversations, such as, 'I have sums to do tonight.' PAUSE 'Daddy was good at sums.' This never fails to make my throat tighten. I still get angry that two young, innocent children could lose their dad so suddenly.

They were both still under five years old when my uncle had a major heart attack and didn't recover. My auntie was in her late thirties and my uncle David was only thirty-seven. He was perfectly fit and healthy, led an active life, and loved his family more than anyone else I know. I think that's why, when we got the phone call, I couldn't believe the bad news. Looking back, I must just have been in shock. It still seems so unfair. Remembering times I spent with him makes me think abut how I saw him – a tall, strong, clever man who never failed to make people laugh. I always looked up to him.

As the kids grow up they remind me more and more of their dad. Connor looks like him in every way and Katie has his bright eyes and sharp mind.

I'm glad I started babysitting for them, as it has taught me to handle situations on my own and I've learned the importance of being responsible. It has also brought me closer to my cousins. I know things about them I would not have known before, like how Connor likes his mango to be cut up, or the order of events is Katie's week.

The best part of babysitting is putting them to bed, especially Connor. I love it when they are all snugly and sleepy, eyes half closed but still insisting I read heir favourite story and do all the voices.

When Connor cosies up to sleep he is hardly any bigger than a pillow, leaving masses of space below on the bed. I tuck him up, smile adoringly at the barely visible lump under the covers and stand for a bit, watching him fall asleep. I think how much I love them both, whisper, 'Night, night' and softly pad down the stairs to wait on the sofa until it's time to go home.

It's probably the most painful thing I've ever done to myself, mentally as well as physically. I should have listened to what my mum told me that day.

I was in the garden playing football by myself. It must have been around eight o'clock when my mum shouted out the window, 'Stop making a racket with that ball! You're going to break something or hurt yourself!' That was one thing I certainly didn't want to do, injure myself. There was a big football competition only a week away and the prize was a Premiership trial with Chelsea.

The next thing I knew I seemed to be running down my driveway diagonally. I just lost my balance and went over on my left ankle with all my weight down upon it. The pain was excruciating. My automatic reaction was to hop onto my still strong foot. If I remember correctly I heard a tearing sound. I knew this couldn't be good.

Casting my mind back I can remember my thoughts and feelings. The second it happened I could feel something ripping and tearing in my ankle. There was unbelievable pain. It was like someone was wrenching my muscles apart and would not stop. I needed to lie down.

I managed to hop back into my house, into the living room and onto the couch. The pain was so sore that I could not even touch my ankle. I was soon, with the help of my mum, lying down with a pack of ice smothered over the ankle.

Days passed. It got no better and so I went to the hospital to be told I would be out of football and all other physical activities for eight weeks. This was where the mental pain lay. I would not be able to take part in the competition.

On top of that, my whole summer holiday was ruined. The pain in my ankle made me feel weak and tired and I knew it was going to be a long eight weeks.

When I look back now on this incident though I realise that it did not actually change or really affect my life. When I think of it I know I had no chance of winning that trial with Chelsea. Sometimes I look back with regret and wonder how far I could have gone, but really I think it was a bit of an unrealistic dream. I still love football but now it's just a hobby to me. The experience hasn't exactly made me a more cautious person, because I still play football every day, but I am more likely to listen to what other people have to say.

I was stupid to keep playing when I was warned to stop. If I had stopped I would have been able to do a lot of great things that summer. I can see now that sometimes what other people tell you or advise you to do is better than your own judgement, and that you should listen to what people say because it might save you from doing something stupid.

I'm sure it's the same on a much wider scale. When you don't listen to people you get yourself hurt, or other people hurt, or you get yourself into trouble.

I hurt my ankle by not listening to my mum, but events like this happen on a much wider and larger scale too. For example people are told not to drink and drive but they do it anyway. When someone is drunk and driving a car they have no control, just like I had no control to stop myself going over on my ankle.

The result of crashing a car drunk is probably hurting someone else as well as yourself, and for sure getting yourself into trouble. That wasn't the case with my ankle. I only hurt myself, but the same moral works on a more serious and wider scale. If you listen to other people, great things can happen and disasters can be avoided.

## Now try this

Now that you have read the stories once, you are going to analyse them in more detail. The easiest way to do this is to have a photocopy of each story in front of you. You'll also need pens, pencils or highlighters in three different colours. You may wish to work with a partner to do the following things as you read the stories again:

1 Every time you find one of the writers sharing their **thoughts or feelings**, underline or highlight that part of the story in your first colour.

2 Every time you find one of the writers using **detail or description**, underline or highlight that part of the story in your second colour.

3 Every time you find one of the writers **being reflective**, underline or highlight that part of the story in your third colour. If you think the writer is **reflecting widely** about life or society, put a capital **W** in the margin beside the highlighted area.

4 Write a couple of sentences for each piece to show what made it a **good** piece of writing.

5 For each piece, suggest two things the writer could have done that would have made their work **even better**.

## Writing your personal reflective piece

First you need to make a plan.

## Now try this

Take a new sheet of paper, at least A4 size. At the top write the task you have chosen. The divide the rest of the page into 4 squares with headings as shown on the next page.

Now use the four squares to plan what you want to put in to your piece of work. Key words, phrases or bullet points will do fine. It's probably easiest if you start with the top left box, where you slot in the rough outline of the story that you're telling. Then go on and fill in the other boxes.

Your title goes here

The basic story

Start

Middle

End

Thoughts and feelings

Details and description

Reflection

## Now try this

If you've chosen Personal Reflective Writing it's now time to write your piece. In class, but under exam conditions and with only your one-page plan to help you, sit down and write your piece. This should take you around an hour to do.

When you've written it, look at the very end of this chapter to find out what to do next.

## Writing to handle ideas

So far in this chapter we have looked at the skills for Personal Reflective Writing because most pupils will do best at that sort of task. However, everybody's mind does not work in the same way, and Personal Reflective Writing really might not be the best thing for you. In that case, you might prefer to write in a way that lets you handle ideas.

This type of writing splits into two main strands.

In **discursive** writing you explore an issue or question. Both sides of the issue are explored, and you will usually give your conclusion at the end, while allowing the reader to decide for himself. In this chapter, whenever we look at the idea of discursive writing, we will do this in the context of a student who has been asked to discuss the issue of whether pupils should be paid to stay on at school after the age of sixteen.

In **persuasive** or **argumentative** writing you start with a clear belief or strongly held point of view. In this kind of text, you will try to use evidence and language to make the reader agree with you. In this chapter, whenever we look at the idea of persuasive writing, we will do this in the context of a student who is arguing that low-cost flights cause many problems.

## Subjects to avoid

Some topics come up again and again. Your teacher has probably read all the arguments about **euthanasia, abortion** and **animal testing** before, and will quickly notice if you miss out anything he or he expects to find, or if there is any important aspect of the argument which you don't explore carefully enough.

Unless you are truly an expert, steer clear of writing about these subjects. And, if you really want to tackle one of these issues, make sure you do it in a two-sided way. Otherwise you'll sound extreme.

## Researching

Whether your piece of writing is one-sided or two-sided, and no matter how much you think you already know about the subject, you need to do some research. Everything you eventually write will be based on this, and it's time well spent.

Nowadays the most likely place to look for information will be on the Internet.

You could visit the websites of charities and pressure groups who have an interest in your topic. If, for example, you are writing about environment issues you could visit the sites of WWF, Greenpeace or Friends of the Earth.

Many newspapers have excellent websites. These can be very useful if your topic has been in the headlines recently, and often give real-life examples you can use. One very good one is www.guardian.co.uk which makes no charge and is easy to access.

Another interesting site is the online encyclopedia www.wikipedia.org which is written by people who use it. This means the contributors are genuinely interested in their subjects. However, some of what they write can be quite biased (as with most published writing). You shouldn't use wikipedia as your only source, but it's good for ideas and examples.

If you don't know which sites you want to use you'll need to begin by using a search engine such as Google. Try to use only one or two keywords for your search. The computer doesn't know what you are thinking, or why you are looking these words up, so be as precise as you can about what you want.

If you're using a phrase, put double quotation marks round it. Looking for "climate change" will find web pages using that complete phrase. This might be just what you want to know:

> **Campaigners against climate change point out that all of the ten hottest years ever recorded have happened in the last fourteen years.**

If you type the same two words without quotation marks you will get all the pages that have the word 'climate' and the word 'change' anywhere on the same page. This isn't so helpful:

**Because the climate was so warm on holiday she had to change her clothes three times a day.**

You might also look in libraries. Ask the staff for advice about the most suitable sources of information. One thing you will find there is an encyclopedia. These can be very good on established factual information, but as huge books like this take many years to write and put together, they are not great sources for material on current controversial topics. For that, you may be better going back to the Internet.

Depending on your topic, you might also speak to people about their own experiences. If you are writing about the rights and wrongs of national service for example, you might want to talk to your grandfather about his time in the army.

## Facts and opinions

Facts can be proved. They are true and nobody can argue against them.

**Chocolate is made of cocoa solids, milk and sugar.**

Opinions are more personal. They are what people think, and different people can have different opinions about the same thing.

**Chocolate is delicious.**

**Chocolate is too sweet.**

## Now try this

Look at the list of sentences below. Which are facts and which are opinions?

1   The most common car colour nowadays is silver.

2   Celtic is a football team.

3   Smoking has an effect on the human body.

4   It's wrong to take part in boxing matches.

5   John F. Kennedy was the best president America ever had.

6   Human cloning is always wrong.

7   Art galleries are boring.

8   Silver cars look sleek and clean.

9   Scientists are very close to being able to carry out human cloning.

10  People who like *Lord of the Rings* are nerds.

11  *Lord of the Rings* was voted the best book of the 20th century.

12  Celtic shouldn't pay huge fees to players' agents.

13  John F. Kennedy was shot and killed in 1963.

14  Teenagers shouldn't smoke.

15  Some boxers suffer brain damage because of their sport.

16  There are four large art galleries in Edinburgh.

## Using facts to support opinions

Once you have collected your facts, you should try to find a way to make each one of them support an opinion.

In **persuasive** writing, organise the facts to support what you believe. In **discursive** writing, organise them to support the two different sides of the argument. Here's an example based on our pupil who is writing persuasively about cheap flights.

> **Fact/example from research**
>
> **The burning of aeroplane fuel is a major cause of climate change.**
>
> **How does this support my opinion?**
>
> **This proves that encouraging people to take more flights is damaging the environment.**

A good writer will be able to 'spin' facts to support their opinion. Two newspapers could have two very different opening sentences at the start of their front-page stories.

> **A development scheme which will turn part of the city centre into a building site, causing months of traffic chaos, was revealed today.**
>
> **A development scheme which will transform a run-down part of the city centre and create hundreds of jobs was revealed today.**

**CHAOS AHEAD!**

**NEW JOBS COME TO AREA**

Both newspapers are reporting the same story, but they have spun the facts to suit heir opinion.

Imagine a man placing a lonely-hearts advert. He's university-educated and has a well-paid job. He enjoys golf and is an expert on wine. He likes eating out and he's forty-five years old. In his advert he might write this:

> **Mature gentleman, well educated, seeks companion for meals out and fine wine.**

## Now try this

Imagine a woman went on a date with him and didn't like him. How might she describe him afterwards? How might she describe their date?

Being able to bend facts towards the direction you want to go is especially useful in persuasive writing when you are trying to make your readers agree with you.

## Structuring your essay

*Planning two-sided, discursive pieces*

In these essays you should show that you understand the arguments on both sides. At the end you can give your opinion, and your readers can decide on theirs.

There are two ways you can structure these essays. We'll look very quickly first at the simple structure. However, it would be better if you used the complex structure, and we'll go in to that in more detail. The **simple structure** works like this:

**Step 1** A one-paragraph introduction to the topic:

**The government wants to encourage more sixteen-year-olds to stay on at school. To encourage this, pupils who return for fifth and sixth year can now be paid to do so.**

**Step 2** A link sentence, explaining which side of the argument you will begin with.

**As a pupil, and therefore someone who might benefit from this plan, I'd like to begin by looking at the reasons why some people believe it to be a good idea.**

**Step 3** Now take all of the points on one side of the argument. Each point should be in a separate paragraph, and these points should be backed up with facts, observations or personal experiences. Use **topic sentences** and the **PEE structure**. (You will find out more about these soon.) Start with the strongest, most convincing arguments and work your way down to the weaker ones. You should aim to have at least three or four paragraphs on the first side of the argument.

**Step 4** Write a link sentence showing that you are about to switch to the other side of the argument.

**I want to turn now to the other side of the argument, and to voice the thoughts of those who do not think pupils should be paid to stay on at school.**

**Step 5**   Now do the same on this side of the argument as you did at Step 3 above, working from the stronger points down to weaker ones.

**Step 6**   Finally, in your conclusion, briefly sum up what you have written. Now say which side you agree with and why. Show which arguments convinced you, or refer to an experience in your life or the life of someone you know which has convinced you that a particular side is right. You may wish to leave the reader with something to think about:

> It is clear that both sides have strong arguments. Having examined them I feel that on the whole it benefits pupils to stay on at school for as long as possible. Anything that encourages someone to get more education and better qualifications is a good thing, so I think the cost of the scheme is money well spent.

The **more complex structure** for two-sided pieces makes you look more skilled at handling your material. It works like this:

The introduction and conclusion are the same as they are in a simply structured essay. However, in the main body of the essay, you begin with the strongest argument from one side of the argument. Then, in the next paragraph, you work through a point on the opposite side that contradicts what you have just written about. Each of these paragraphs will use topic sentences and the PEE structure, which will be explained later in this chapter.

> Perhaps the strongest argument for paying young people to stay on at school is that it stops them leaving to get a job. In lower-income families, there may be a lot of pressure on teenagers, even very bright ones, to leave school and go out to work as soon as possible to bring some money into the house.

However, this assumes that poorer parents just view their teenagers as a source of income. This is an insult to these families. All good parents want their children to do well and get qualifications. They know that school is already giving their children something very valuable – a good education.

Then take the second strongest point from the first side of the argument. Explain it, and then challenge it by making another point from the opposite side to contradict it. Keep going, following this pattern.

You may find that some of your points cannot be paired up in this way. You can deal with them just before you start your conclusion. All the remaining points can be rolled into two short paragraphs, one for the ideas which support one side of the argument, for example:

There are some other good reasons why many people think that pupils should be paid to stay on at school . . .

and the other for the evidence that matches the other side of the argument, for example:

Those who are against this plan also have some further reasons for their position . . .

## Structuring persuasive writing

Organising persuasive writing is very similar, but simpler. In persuasive writing you don't have to switch from one part of the argument to the other, because you are always trying to defend your point of view.

**Step 1**  A one-paragraph introduction to the topic. Make clear straight away what you believe about the subject. Use your wit and passion to grab the reader's attention from the start.

Our skies are filling with brightly coloured planes. We seem to have become so used to them that we never question their place in our lives. However I firmly believe Britain would be a better place if we put an end to budget airlines and their cheap flights.

**Step 2**   Using the points you've planned, set out your argument. Each point should be in a separate paragraph, and these points should be backed up with facts, observations or personal experiences. Use **topic sentences** and the **PEE structure**. (You will find out more about these soon.) Start with the strongest, most convincing arguments and work your way down to the weaker ones.

> **Apart from a few clueless Americans, everyone accepts that the world's climate is changing. What's more, everyone agrees the rate of change is itself speeding up. It's surely no coincidence that the frightening phenomenon of global warming has become so much worse in the decade since cheap flights took to the sky. Aviation fuel is a major source of highly polluting carbons. Take these planes out of the sky and we give the earth a chance to cool down again.**

Although you are always defending your own position in this kind of writing, your argument will be stronger if you can show that you understand the other side's position and can argue against it.

> **You might be wondering how people will cope if we suddenly take these budget airlines out of the sky. Surely people need access to transport? Of course they do. First of all, my law would simply be that no airline can charge less than £100 for a single journey. This would make people carefully consider whether they actually need to make a trip. If they feel they have to travel, a flight is still possible. However they may decide to either stay at home, or to travel by another means. A huge amount of pollution would be prevented. As the number of flights from Britain gradually declined, people would spend more holidays here, boosting our economy.**

**Step 3**   You may find that some of your points are not strong enough to be dealt with in their own separate paragraph. If you still feel they are valuable and want to use them, then you can deal with them just before you start your conclusion. All the remaining points can be rolled into one short paragraph:

> **There are some other good reasons why I believe that budget airlines are a menace . . .**

**Step 4**   Finally, in your conclusion, briefly sum up what you have written. End with a strong, clear statement that shows again why you believe you are right. You may also want to challenge the reader to think or respond.

Putting an end to cheap flights would make the world a better place. We'd breathe in less pollution, appreciate our own country more, spend our money more thoughtfully, and we'd be doing our bit for the planet. Do you really need to climb into a tin box to go on your next holiday?

## Structuring your paragraphs

As well as structuring and ordering your whole essay, you need to have a clear structure in each paragraph. The best way to do this is to use **topic sentences**, and **the PEE pattern**.

### Topic sentences

A topic sentence is called this for two reasons.

1   It refers to the topic of the essay.

2   It introduces the topic of its paragraph.

The topic sentence is usually the first in the paragraph. Look at the following paragraph from our anti-cheap-flights writer. The topic sentence has been underlined. The words that tie that sentence in to the topic of the whole essay are in bold.

<u>Of course another vital reason for **putting an end to cheap flights** is that they take all the enjoyable anticipation out of travel.</u> If it costs a few hundred pounds to go somewhere, then people will research their destination, plan their journey, and maybe even save up for the ticket. If you can go somewhere for £1.99 it doesn't matter if you've never heard of the place; you'll go on the spur of the moment without having the enjoyment of looking forward to your time there.

*Using PEE*

Within each paragraph of your essay, apart from the introduction and conclusion, you should try to use the **PEE** structure. It goes like this:

P     Make a **Point** that is relevant to the topic of your essay. This point is the topic sentence at the start of the paragraph.

> **One reason young people should be encouraged to stay on at school is that there are very few jobs you can now get without good qualifications.**

E     Give **Evidence** to back up the point you are making. This should be either a fact you found out during your research, something you have noticed, or something you have experienced yourself.

> **As part of my research for this essay I examined twenty job adverts taken at random from our local evening paper. Eighteen of them asked for a particular qualification. Sixteen asked for applicants to have a certain amount of experience.**

E     **Explain** this. If you are writing to persuade, show how it adds to your argument. If you are doing a piece of discursive writing, show how the point and evidence contribute to this side of the topic.

> **This seems to show that staying on at school is something all teenagers should be encouraged to do and will benefit from. Paying pupils to do so would be one way of getting them to take part in further study.**

## Direction markers

Certain words and phrases signal the direction of the argument in a piece of discursive writing, or emphasise the writer's point of view in persuasive writing. Most of these words and phrases appear at the start of a paragraph or sentence.

Some words and phrases move the argument forwards:

> **Next, I'd like to deal with the issues caused by airport expansion.**

> **Also, cheap airlines tend to treat their customers like cattle.**

Some words and phrases let the argument change direction:

> **Nevertheless, there are those who say that cheap flights are a way of allowing people to broaden their minds and their experience.**

**Despite this**, many would say that nobody should be paid to take up an education which is already costly for taxpayers and free for pupils and parents.

Some words and phrases can be used in summing up:

**In conclusion**, cheap flights are a menace.

**To summarise**, each side has strong arguments.

Some words and phrases show that the writer is sure he is right:

It is **absolutely** clear that pollution is increasing

It is **indubitably** time for us to start worrying about the impact of cheap flights.

## Now try this

Look at these four headings:

- These expressions move the argument forwards

- These expressions let the argument change direction

- These expressions allow the writer to sum up

- These expressions show the writer is sure he is right

Now look at the expressions below and over the page. Each one fits best under one of the above headings. Write each heading at the top of a different piece of paper. Underneath the heading, list the expressions that fit there. Check any new words with a dictionary as you go.

| | | | |
|---|---|---|---|
| nonetheless | rather | in contrast | instead |
| without a doubt | undeniably | surely | definitely |
| thus | otherwise | moreover | yet |
| nevertheless | finally | on the contrary | obviously |
| likewise | conversely | on the other hand | whereas |
| unquestionably | therefore | however | next |
| despite | similarly | in spite of | absolutely |
| at the same time | without question | and | alternatively |
| in retrospect | without doubt | significantly | |

| | | | |
|---|---|---|---|
| *in conclusion* | *first(ly)* | *accordingly* | *but* |
| *also* | *in brief* | *second(ly)* | *although* |
| *in addition* | *furthermore* | *as a result* | *indubitably* |
| *consequently* | *third(ly)* | *because* | *equally* |
| *on the whole* | *to sum up* | *to balance this* | |
| *what is more* | *in other words* | *certainly* | |

If you want to refer to another argument so you can knock it down, two useful words are *claim* and *allege*. They hint that you do not believe something the other side says.

The well-known racing driver *claims* to have a clean licence and never to have been caught speeding.

His enemies *allege* that he spent years in a foreign prison for drug smuggling. He however *claims* that he was framed after he refused to pay a bribe to customs officers at the border.

Some words are useful if you can't prove something for sure. These words are also usual for suggestions and rumours. These words include **reported, rumoured, believed, could, likely, would** and **may point to**. For example, here's a piece of gossip that may have very few provable facts behind it:

It is **believed** that troubled TV presenter Warren Way **could** again be struggling with the marriage problems originally **reported** last year. It is **rumoured** that his rows with his former glamour model wife Syria **could have** risen to as many as four a day. It is **likely** that the Wonder Wedding Dating Agency, who pay him £1million a year to be the face of their 'Happy Hearts Make Happy Homes' campaign **would be** very unhappy to have a spokesman whose marriage was on the skids. The TV star's close friends are **reported** to be very concerned. Way's non-appearance on last night's edition of How Mean Is Your Spouse? **may point to** continuing problems in his stormy relationship with the curvaceous Syria.

## Persuasive techniques

In persuasive writing you should be writing about a topic you are personally interested in and know about. The key here is to use facts and experiences to put across a series of points that support something you believe. Your aim is to persuade the reader to agree with you.

This type of approach often works well with topics that allow you to use humour or even sarcasm. 'Why reality TV is rubbish' is an ideal subject, for example, whereas more serious topics really deserve the two-sided, discursive approach.

Persuasive writing tends to use certain techniques. Some of the most common are:

- **repetition** of words or phrases

- dramatic-sounding **short sentences**

- including the reader by using **'we' and related words**

- asking **rhetorical questions** – which do not need an answer but make the reader think

- an **appeal to the reader's emotions,** or **emotive language** which stirs up the readers' feelings

- offering the reader a **vision** of success or achievement.

## Now try this

To see these persuasive techniques in use, read the following text. It is for a speech to a class. How many examples can you find of each technique being used?

How would you like to stand out from the crowd? How would you like to be remembered? How would you like to become more famous?

All this can be achieved if you join me. I want us, all of us, to sit down in Princes Street and bring Edinburgh to a halt.

Think of it. Imagine it. Picture it. We could be walking past the shops as normal, blending in with the rest of the crowd. Then suddenly, when the lights are at red, we'll pour on to the pedestrian crossing and sit down.

Think of the power. We'll be in control of the traffic. We'll be in control of the centre of Edinburgh. We'll have the eyes of the media up on us as they try to find out why we've done this.

You might think, 'Won't the police just drag us away?' No – because they won't dare lay hands on a group of teenagers, especially if we put he youngest, prettiest girls on the outside of the group. You might say, 'Won't we get arrested?' I'm asking you to sit in the road, not to break shop windows or threaten drivers.

Just picture us as we sit there. Think of how famous we will be. We'll be talked about forever after, the teenagers who took control of a capital city and demanded that people pay us some attention at last.

## Now try this

If you've chosen Discursive or Persuasive Writing it's now time to write your piece. In class, but under exam conditions, sit down and write your piece. This should take you around an hour to do.

## Now try this

When you've finished, read your work over before you hand it in to your teacher. Think about the four areas you will be assessed on and ask yourself the following questions:

**Content**

■ Have I stuck to my task?

■ Have I developed my ideas?

**Structure**

■ Is my work organised, straightforward, and clear to follow?

**Expression**

■ Have I followed the guidelines in this chapter about the genre of writing I'm attempting?

■ Have I used good vocabulary and different sorts of sentences?

■ Is my point of view clear?

**Technical accuracy**

■ Are my spelling, grammar and punctuation the best I can possibly achieve?

Once you have checked your work, hand it in to your teacher.

## What happens next?

Your teacher will mark your work and let you know if it's good enough. If it is, you will have passed and that is the end of this NAB. If it still needs some improvement, your teacher should advise you what needs to be changed.